Swimming
Upstream

PATSY PERIL grew up in the fishing community of Coonagh, on the outskirts of Limerick city. He has been involved in the inland fisheries all his life. He is also an experienced light aircraft pilot.

Since childhood, Patsy has been deeply concerned with environmental matters, in particular concerning the health and future of Irish rivers. For decades, he has been involved in organisations engaged with the oversight, protection and reclamation of our natural environment and its sustainable use. He has long been a member of both local and national salmon net fishers' associations in Ireland, serving as Chair of the Net Fishers' Association in 2006. From 1992 to 2008, he was a member of the Shannon Regional Fisheries Board and from 2000 to 2005 a member of the National Salmon Commission. From 1993 to 2023, he served as Chair of the Sea Fishers' Advisory Group to the Irish Seal Sanctuary and as a representative for the Irish Seal Sanctuary at meetings of the North Atlantic Salmon Conservation Organisation, an international, intercontinental body with direct government inputs.

Still based in Coonagh, and at an age when many would have fully retired, Patsy Peril continues his activism, striving for a time when our natural waterways are respected and cared for, and for a healthy and sustainable balance between traditional use of our environment, and its wellbeing and natural balance. A frequent contributor to meetings, conferences and congresses, Patsy is now ready to bring his crucial message to a general readership.

DEIRDRE NUTTALL has over twenty years' experience of interview-led collaborative writing projects in the areas of memoir, biography, academic writing and popular non-fiction. Among the many memoirs she has collaborated on for the mass market, Paul Connolly's *Against All Odds* (John Blake, 2010) was a bestseller, and Lisa Lawlor's *Stardust Baby* (Mirror, 2021) was a bestseller in the Irish market. Her own academic volume *Different and the Same: A Folk History of the Protestants of Independent Ireland* (Eastwood, 2020) was one of the *Irish Independent*'s books of the year.

Deirdre has a strong academic background. She holds a PhD in ethnology and a master's degree in Social Anthropology, with expertise in narrative, oral history and the ethnology of symbolic thought and practice.

Swimming Upstream

One man's fight to save the Atlantic wild salmon

PATSY PERIL with DEIRDRE NUTTALL

THE O'BRIEN PRESS
DUBLIN

First published in 2024 by
The O'Brien Press Ltd,
12 Terenure Road East, Rathgar, Dublin 6, D06 HD27 Ireland.
Tel: +353 1 4923333; Fax: +353 1 4922777
E-mail: books@obrien.ie
Website: obrien.ie
The O'Brien Press is a member of Publishing Ireland

ISBN: 978-1-78849-478-6

8 7 6 5 4 3 2 1
28 27 26 25 24

Picture section credits
Irish Independent, courtesy of the National Library of Ireland: page 1 (both);
Johnny Woodlock: pages 7 (both), 8 (top); Dr William O'Connor: page 8 (bottom).
All other photographs courtesy of the Peril family.

Printed and bound in Poland by Bialostockie Zaklady Graficzne S.A.
The paper in this book is produced using pulp from managed forests.

Published in

Dedication

In memory of Gabriel and of all the souls who lost their
lives on the great River Shannon.

Acknowledgements

This book would not have happened without the support of Brendan and Mary Price, and of the Irish Seal Sanctuary in general. Thank you all. Thanks also to Bairbre ní Fhloinn for introducing us and suggesting that we could work together on this book.

A number of archives and other sources were consulted in the process of writing, and we would like to thank in particular the staff of Moyross Public Library, Limerick; and of Limerick Archives at Lissanalty, who provided access to the very valuable minutes of Limerick no. 8 Fishery District Management Board meetings, and Limerick Harbour Board operations. A big thank you to Ken Bergin of the Special Collections Library at the University of Limerick, who facilitated full study access to the salmon fishing records section and to the family papers donated to the library by the Knight of Glin. Thanks to the National Folklore Collection at UCD, and to the National Library of Ireland, whose collections were invaluable. A big thanks to the Military Archives in Cathal Brugha Army Barracks for their kindness in making available some very special records pertaining to the history of the Peril family.

Finally, a sincere thank you to the O'Brien Press for sharing our vision for this book and our hope that it will make a difference.

Patsy Peril

Deirdre Nuttall

CONTENTS

Preface

Unlike me, the Atlantic wild salmon does not have a voice, so it cannot tell the story of why and how it has been driven to the point of extinction. As one of the last remaining traditional fishermen of the Shannon, and someone who derived a decent livelihood and lifestyle from the commercial exploitation of salmon, I feel that it behoves me to sound the warning, to give a voice to a species that has given me everything.

I am a salmon fisherman, the son of a fisherman and a native of an area whose fortunes over the years have been linked intimately with the fate of the Atlantic wild salmon. From my home in Coonagh, I have seen at first hand the degradation of its environment in Ireland, in parallel with the loss of the traditional way of life of the fishing families. The same story has been playing out all over the North Atlantic region. I have fought for years to see sustainable policies put in place to save the salmon before it is too late. I have done my very best to speak out, although it often seems that what I say is falling on deaf ears.

I am here to tell you now that we have a short window of opportunity to save this iconic species. In the process, we can also improve the health of our entire marine ecosystem and of the rural communities that depend on it. That time is rapidly running out.

My own life, my family history on the shores of the Shannon, the fate of the salmon and how the Irish State has treated our environment all run in parallel, and are impossible to discuss separately. So in these pages, I can only speak of all these things together.

CHAPTER ONE

Electrification

In December 1922, the Irish Free State was born, and in May 1923, the Civil War that followed independence came to an end. The new nation had plenty of pressing matters to attend to: the rebuilding of central Dublin; the healing of communities that had been torn apart; the development of a land that was then one of the poorest areas of western Europe; and the fostering of a sense of nationhood among a traumatised population, to mention just a few.

One urgent issue was electrification. Ireland lagged far behind the rest of western Europe and much of the developed world in this respect. Most rural and many urban and suburban areas still had no electricity. Without a modern network, Ireland would remain unable to industrialise and develop. We would forever be dependent on Britain, which was then by far our biggest export market, as well as a major destination for enormous numbers of Irish people who emigrated and migrated every year in search of opportunity.

At that time, in those parts of Ireland that did have electricity, it was largely provided by small private suppliers, about 300 in total. Roughly three-quarters of the nation's electricity was used in the Dublin area.[1] Many rural people had never experienced electricity at all, and could hardly imagine its potential to change the way they lived. At a glance, it was not at all obvious how Ireland was going to turn this situation around. While many other countries relied chiefly on coal-burning power stations, and had their own mining industries to provide the precious fuel, Ireland had no coal reserves, and had always relied on imports from Britain. But there were other possibilities, notably the vast energy embodied by the River Shannon, one of the largest rivers in Europe, vast and deep and wide and full of largely untapped potential.

The Shannon is by far the biggest river in Ireland, 360 kilometres long with a catchment area estimated to amount to about one-eighth of the country. It flows through Lough Allen, Lough Ree, and Lough Derg on its way to the sea near Limerick. The Shannon Estuary with its brackish water, subject to the movement of the tides, extends over 100 kilometres inland. Talk of harnessing the power of the Shannon had been ongoing since the early nineteenth century, but nothing had been done about it.

In 1835, CW Williams addressed the British parliament, referring to the remarkable poverty of many Irish in the western part of the country – 'absolutely wanting the necessaries of life, and driven to desperation'; 'miserable people' – and the pattern of huge numbers migrating to Britain for work. Williams pointed out that the Shannon, the largest river in Britain and Ireland, remained undeveloped and had the potential to utterly transform the fortunes of the western half of Ireland. He further said that the waterways of Canada – still a British colony and much more distant from the centres of power than Ireland – were comparatively well-developed.[2] The Shannon was an important transport artery and fishery throughout the nineteenth century, and it clearly had potential for much greater exploitation.

Nothing much happened in the following decades, and the extraordinary levels of poverty and emigration witnessed by Williams would – shamefully – remain a feature of life in the western parts of Ireland for generations to come, persisting well into my own lifetime.

In the early 1920s, a young Irish electrical engineer called Thomas McLaughlin was working in Germany, then a leader in the development of complex engineering infrastructures. Thomas studied all the options on the table for the electrification of Ireland, and determined that the power of the River Shannon represented the best possible means of providing a nationwide supply of electricity. He took his ideas to the Irish government, and the government listened. Although the project was going to cost an enormous amount of money, at a time when the country's rulers were still learning how to govern and when money was very much lacking, it decided to act decisively and quickly.

In 1924, Herr Reichard and Herr Wallem, principal engineers at the German firm Siemens-Schuckert and world experts in hydroelectricity, visited Ireland. They viewed the Shannon and spoke with Irish government authorities about how the river might be used to electrify the country.[3] All of this convinced the government – in particular Patrick McGilligan, Minister for Industry and Commerce from 1925 and also an old college pal of Thomas's from University College Dublin[4] – that this was the right approach.

The Free State made an agreement with Siemens-Schuckert for the German company to oversee the creation of a vast new hydroelectrical plant with the potential to push Ireland into the industrial age and turn its fortunes around. The project would be known as the Shannon Scheme. It was so huge, so ambitious and so fascinating that, even though the country was still reeling from the recent years of violence, the very idea of it filled newspaper pages and people's heads with astonishing new thoughts.

Critics of the Shannon Scheme – including Éamon de Valera, who was then in opposition[5] – pointed out that Ireland was not an industrial country. It was relatively poor and underdeveloped, with large numbers still employed in traditional, small-scale farming, using techniques that had remained essentially unchanged since the Middle Ages. It was suggested that there really wouldn't be great interest in electricity in rural areas and villages, and that perhaps a ready supply of electricity was not that important to Ireland, or at least not yet. Perhaps it would make more sense to leave such a major infrastructural project until Ireland had developed further, when poverty was less of an issue, and when the government had more money to invest.

Supporters of the Shannon Scheme quickly countered that there were 130 towns and sizeable villages in the country with no electricity at all. Goods that had once been made by hand in Ireland and sold locally were now being replaced by industrially produced items imported from overseas, and at a time of high emigration.[6] If Ireland was to have any future at all, they argued, it needed to improve its industrial base, and the only way to do that was with a reliable source of electricity.

In 1925, the Dáil passed the Shannon Electricity Act, providing for a power plant at Ardnacrusha, near Limerick, and giving the government sweeping powers to do whatever it took to get the plant built. A contract was signed with Siemens-Schuckert in August of that year.[7] It was anticipated that the scheme would have a dramatic impact on the fish living in the Shannon, but the Act made no provision for the welfare of the river's biodiversity or the preservation of the salmon fisheries. Both were considered a price worth paying at that time, even though many communities depended on the fisheries to survive. Construction on the Shannon Scheme began in September that year.

Nowadays, before engaging in a project of this nature, it would be necessary to carry out comprehensive environmental-impact studies. The threat to the natural environment would be assessed, and steps would be detailed to mitigate against this. But in those days, no such studies were required. If they had been, though less was known then about biodiversity and conservation than now, many glitches in the operation of the service could have been avoided, and many issues that are still ongoing to this day could have been solved. While we cannot judge the people of the past by the standards of today, it is fair to say that the Irish authorities, in their rush to build the hydroelectric plant, simply bypassed elementary planning and safety compliance, even by the lower standards of their time.

In 1927, the Dáil passed the Electricity Supply Act, 'to make provision for the transmission, distribution, and supply of electricity'.[8] The Electricity Supply Board (ESB) was established to operate the Shannon Power Works and to organise a national supply of electricity,[9] in what would be the world's first entirely integrated national electricity utility.[10]

Having inspected various options, the electrical engineers decided to use the total fall of the hydraulic gradient from Lough Derg to Limerick. In order to capture the full potential energy of the 100-foot difference in water levels, the engineers constructed a major dam at Parteen Villa, six kilometres south of Lough Derg and Killaloe. It extends across the main Shannon River, from County Clare to Birdhill in County Tipperary. Impounding the river in this way enabled the diversion or abstraction of the water at the dam into a twelve-kilometre aqueduct race, giving a

100-foot head of water gravity to the turbines at Ardnacrusha power station. The expended water that ends up in the tail race, after the generating process, is very unlike the gentle water of the head race. In fact, the powerful forces of nature released in the process still have to be seen – and heard – to be believed.

The huge Ardnacrusha plant, constructed in reinforced concrete,[11] incorporated the German technique known as the Caisson method, a form of geotechnical engineering involving pre-cast concrete elements.[12] A two-kilometre tail-race canal was blasted through the rock to route the diverted water back to the River Shannon above Limerick City, through which a broad stretch of the river flows. In the process, two rivers were diverted, and four new bridges – three on the head race and one on the tail race – were constructed where the intake canal and tail race cut across roads.[13] The need of water-based life to travel was wilfully neglected. No fish pass was provided, despite there already being a very good understanding of the importance of passes around obstacles such as weirs and dams.

However, the dam built at the power station did include a boat pass of unique design – a double-stepped navigation lock inside an enclosed tower, incorporated into the dam itself. When flooded, it raised a boat about halfway up in the first chamber, from whence it could proceed into the next chamber. This would then be sealed from the first by watertight doors and flooded, raising the boat to the level of the head race. The boat could descend to the tail race by reversing the process.

The work on the Shannon Scheme was on an epic scale, and involved the transformation of huge swathes of the natural landscape. The work site was sixteen kilometres long. Building had to take place both in the water and on land, at a time before most of the machinery that is now standard for such work had been invented. A railway system was built to support the construction works. It would carry 23,000 cubic metres of timber, 65,000 tons of cement, 2670 tons of steel to reinforce the concrete, 110,000 tons of coal and 700 tons of explosives.[14] For the construction of the power station at Ardnacrusha alone, workers had to excavate about 350,000 cubic metres of earth and rock, most of which was recycled for use elsewhere in the project.[15]

The Shannon Scheme was, of course, a huge employer. A temporary village was built for the German staff overseeing and working on the project, where many lived with their wives and children. Vast numbers of Irish labourers and other workers were also employed. In September 1925, the government advertised in the national press for 3000 unskilled workers – mostly very young, strong men, whose muscle was required to dig channels out of the rock. The same rock would be mixed with cement to build walls, dykes and dams – offering thirty-two shillings for a fifty-two-hour week, including free accommodation and access to canteens where food would be sold cheaply.[16] While the pay was a pittance, it was enough during those troubled economic times to attract workers from all over the country. The decision to align the wage rate with the pay received by agricultural labourers was deliberate: even in Ireland, industrial workers were increasingly inclined to organise themselves into unions. There was a lot of anxiety about communism among employers and other people of influence, including the Church, and memories of the big workers' strike in Dublin, the Lockout of 1913, were still fresh.

Many labourers came from Galway, with large numbers from rural and Gaeltacht areas, which were still wracked with poverty and extremely high rates of emigration. A substantial proportion of the workers came from small farming and labouring backgrounds. Safety signs were erected in German, English and Irish, and all three languages were heard on-site daily.[17]

At its peak, over four thousand men, mostly semi-skilled workers and labourers, were employed at the Ardnacrusha construction site. The accommodation provided was insufficient, with some having to rent spaces to sleep in local farmers' barns, cowsheds and piggeries. So many stayed at the townland of Ballykeelaun – near St Thomas Island, just outside Limerick – that it was compared to an Irish Klondike.[18]

The work, much of it carried out with nothing more sophisticated than picks, shovels and brute force, was very tough and very dangerous. Labourers started at half-past seven in the morning, had an hour for lunch, and finished at half-past six. Every second week, they had to work the night shift. Each worker was assigned a number, which was printed on a disc to hang around his neck. Meals were extremely basic: tea with bread and butter for breakfast; meat, vegetables and potatoes for dinner in the middle of the day; and tea with bread and jam for the evening meal.[19] There were lots of injuries, for which 1249 workers received at least some degree of compensation.

In this tough, gruelling environment, the labourers from Galway were considered the toughest, wildest and hardest-working. It was said that most of them had only one set of clothes, and that at the end of a day's work, covered in mud, they would wade into the freezing waters of the Shannon to clean themselves and their clothing.

Public interest in the building of the Shannon Scheme was massive, as nothing of the sort had ever been attempted in Ireland before. It was rewarding for the people of Ireland to contemplate this bold new project at a time when so many were recovering from the trauma and upset of the previous decade of conflicts. Thousands of people from all over the country travelled to Limerick to see the enormous construction site, to marvel at the immense workforce and imagine what Ireland would be like when the project was completed. In June 1928, for example, a group of about seven hundred, on a trip from Galway to Limerick arranged by the Jesuit Fathers, visited the Ardnacrusha work site en masse and pronounced themselves highly impressed.[20]

The construction site had become a temporary tourist attraction. This was a big coup for the public relations efforts of the ESB, which was running a campaign to educate the public on what Ardnacrusha was going to achieve. They offered reduced train fares to Limerick, regular bus tours, and a nationwide advertising campaign.

The claiming of the Shannon by the Free State was not just a practical matter, but also a powerful symbolic act. Writing in the *Journal of the Royal Society of Arts* in 1927, George Fletcher said that it was 'an economic and psychological gesture that Ireland was going to change her methods and come into line with modern views of life and modern methods of life, both agricultural and industrial,' and 'a new starting-ground for the Irish people'. The enterprise would 'electrify' the minds of the Irish at the same time as it electrified their businesses and homes.[21]

For years during the colonial period, fishing and other rights to the river had been held by big landowners like the Earl of Desmond. Local people were only allowed to use the water in limited and strictly policed ways, reminding them every day that although this might be their home, they were not in charge. Salmon rivers had long been a significant source of wealth to the landlord class. Large quantities of Irish salmon were exported – 900 tons in 1689 – when many of the ordinary people went hungry.[22]

Now Ireland was ruled by the Irish, and the newly independent country was taking a huge step towards modernisation, working to exploit the country's biggest river, and doing so on its own terms. This was a powerfully emotional matter – the reclaiming of a resource that had been seen for centuries as being exploited unfairly.

The ESB was so proud of its achievements that it hired Seán Keating, the famous Limerick painter, to record the work in progress in artistic form.[23] In 1927, Franklin D Roosevelt, then governor of the state of New York, wrote of his interest in the scheme and in the nationalisation of electricity.[24] In May 1929, *Scientific American* published a glowing, fully-illustrated article covering the works, portraying Ireland as a plucky, feisty, forward-thinking small nation taking tangible steps towards modernisation and progress. Gratifyingly, the British media also published ample photo reportage of the 'modern marvel of engineering' that the Irish government hoped would soon power the entire state,[25] heralding 'a new dawn for industrial Erin'.[26]

Some British journalists did – of course – take the opportunity to get in a dig at the 'lazy' Irish. On 19 January 1929, one newspaper published a photograph of German and Irish employees on the project, and stated that the 'somewhat indolent natives' had been 'staggered by Teutonic efficiency', and that the power station would be of huge benefit to Ireland only 'if the populace is sufficiently wealthy to utilise its electricity'.[27]

But most Irish people, wealthy or not, were keenly aware of how a ready supply of electricity would make their lives easier. In December 1928, a Miss Cole, Secretary of the Irish Women's Electrical Association, which had been founded by Thomas McLaughlin's wife, Olwen,[28] gave a public lecture on the wonders of electricity. She described how it would make life easier for busy women in the home, who would soon be using 'all the wonderful advantages that are enjoyed by the most progressive countries'. Domestic electricity, she stated, could power up to six pieces of apparatus at any one time,[29] a truly marvellous thought.

The completed building at Ardnacrusha was genuinely impressive: a German-designed building of immense size, with tall windows and steep-pitched roofs, the style was typical of industrial Berlin, not rural Ireland, where there was very little industry and most people lived in modest homes.[30]

The official opening of the plant, by President of the Executive Council of the Irish Free State WT Cosgrave, took place on 22 July 1929. Reverend Fogarty, Bishop of Killaloe, blessed the project, and Cosgrave then pressed a button that diverted the Shannon waters into the six-mile canal feeding the turbines to bring their momentous, almost frightening, power to life.[31]

And just like that, the terrible beauty that is the Ardnacrusha power station was born. And nothing, in all sorts of ways, was ever the same again.

After the official opening of the power station, the scale of works on the Shannon Scheme was a little smaller than before, but expansion of the site continued, with reduced but still considerable numbers of men continuing to provide general labour. Even as work continued post-opening, the Shannon Scheme was hailed internationally as a tremendous success.

The Irish government basked in the glory, congratulating itself for being so forward-thinking (even though, the same year that Ardnacrusha opened, the Censorship of Publications bill was passed in the Dáil, having a chilling effect on free speech that would linger for decades). From October 1930 to February 1931, letter writers could purchase a special commemorative stamp issued to mark Ireland's great achievement, while various private postcard producers sold picture postcards of the installation.[32] In 1931, several American newspapers published a cartoon showing a pretty Irish 'colleen' gazing happily at the Ardnacrusha plant from her cottage door, with the legend, 'If St Patrick Could Only See That.'[33]

By 1932, about 185,000 day-trippers, or about six per cent of the population of the country, had visited and marvelled at Ardnacrusha.[34] That same year, Ireland hosted the Eucharistic Congress, an enormous spectacle including the Papal Nuncio and thousands of visiting clerics and religious tourists. The Congress, featuring public worship on a grand scale, was celebrated in great style in the Limerick area. The Limerick Development Association requested that the local business community observe 27 June as a holiday, and urged local businesses and citizens to adorn the streets with suitable decorations. The city of Limerick and smaller communities all over the county were decorated lavishly with flags, religious imagery, altars, and grottoes, and about eight thousand people from the Limerick area travelled to Dublin for the festivities.[35]

The Congress was executed with remarkable efficiency and aplomb, and received huge attention from the world's media. While the American cartoon of the colleen mentioned above suggested that traditional Irish Catholicism and technological innovation were at odds with one another, it seemed the Irish government was doing an excellent job at showing that they were not.

By 1936/7, Ardnacrusha was providing 87 per cent of Ireland's electrical requirements,[36] and was clearly a success. It had been a huge publicity coup for the Free State, showing everyone that it could fund, organise and execute one of the most impressive modern feats of engineering in the world, even as Ireland adjusted to self-governance. It was also – as we will see – an absolute disaster for the salmon, other species in and on the Shannon and the environment in general.

The saddest thing about the environmental fallout of the Shannon Scheme is that it was no surprise. The government knew from the beginning that the hydroelectric plant was going to have a catastrophic effect on the environment, and very consciously did almost nothing about it. In 1930, when the Shannon Scheme was nearing completion, the board of the Limerick division of the Inland Fisheries of Ireland organisation demanded that the Department of Fisheries hold an inquiry into what bye-laws were required for the protection of fish. It was already very evident that the works had seriously compromised their ability to navigate the river and therefore to reproduce.[37]

From even before its opening, the Ardnacrusha power station was an important actor in Ireland's history. A hero in the story of Ireland's industrialisation, but a villain in a sad tale of environmental loss and degradation. My own family's story has been intimately linked to the Shannon Scheme and the Ardnacrusha power station ever since, and so has that of the Atlantic wild salmon.

※ ※ ※

Salmon fishing has been central to the economies of the Atlantic region for thousands of years, and has been subject to formal legislation and scientific interest for almost as long. A cave near the Vézère River in France contains a drawing dating to about 20,000 BC that depicts a man holding an Atlantic salmon. In Ireland, it probably also dates back as far as the Mesolithic Age, when the first human settlers fished our rivers, seas and the Atlantic Ocean. In 1987, a possibly ancient dugout canoe was found on the bank of the River Fergus, a tributary of the Shannon, at Clenagh, just a few miles from

Coonagh. In the first century AD, the first-known scientific writing on salmon was penned by Pliny the Elder in his work *Natural Histories*.[38]

By the early Middle Ages, salmon fishing in Atlantic Europe was big business, and strictly enforced rules and regulations were gradually introduced to protect it. In the eleventh century, rulers in England passed laws banning salmon fishing during the breeding season. By the thirteenth century, weirs had been observed to cause problems for the salmon, and the Magna Carta of 1215 – a royal charter of rights agreed to by King John of England – demanded the removal of weirs throughout England, leading to a rebound in the salmon population.

Few industries in the Middle Ages and the early modern period were subject to more legislation than salmon fishing. This shows how important the salmon fisheries were, and also that people in those times already had a reasonably good understanding of the species' vulnerabilities. They knew how to protect the salmon, despite having little or no understanding of where they went at sea, and what they did when they got there.

At around the time of the Magna Carta in England, Irish fishermen were starting to employ snap nets. These were short nets, about ten metres long, stretched out between two small river-fishing boats. Snap nets were introduced to Ireland by the Normans, initially in the area of the Barrow, Nore and Suir in the east of the country. They spread from there to other regions,[39] and snap nets were still in use in parts of the Shannon Estuary in the mid-twentieth century.

A civil survey of Ireland was carried out in 1654–56, recording that, at the time, there were eight sites with fishing weirs in the Shannon Estuary, one of which was at Coonagh.[40] The Coonagh fishermen utilised a range of techniques for catching salmon. Writing in 1832, WH Maxwell describes the estuary fishermen's technique, by which five or six men in a boat with nets were capable of capturing up to five hundred salmon at a time.[41] In 1836, they were recorded as using stake nets – vertical walls of netting held up by lines of strong wooden poles, interrupting the natural course of the fish to direct them into the net – and bag nets.[42] This technique would remain in use until the 1960s.

In 1863, the Salmon Fisheries Act was passed, a counterpart of legislation passed for England and Wales in 1861. This reduced the number of fixed structures such as weirs on rivers, removing some of the pressure from the Irish salmon stock. The Act divided Ireland into seventeen fisheries districts, each with its own board of conservators.[43] The Limerick area, incorporating Coonagh, was designated district number 8. From 1864, fishermen were also using drift nets, which required a licence. Drift nets are suspended in the water, anywhere from just below the surface to the bottom of the riverbed.

Despite all this fishing, there were still lots of salmon in the Shannon, and the fisheries were a very important element of the economy. In 1877, about fifteen thousand salmon were caught every year on the Shannon's Lax Weir, near Limerick. Throughout the 1870s, Irish salmon rivers generated about £400,000 worth of income annually, an enormous sum in those days.[44]

In the years before the First World War, when material for nets was scarce, only 100 licenses were given out annually, and their use was strictly enforced, which could cause resentment. The number of drift-net licences dropped again after the completion of the Shannon Scheme, with just a small, temporary move upwards during the Second World War, when some foods were in short supply, and prices for salmon were high.[45] In the 1940s, the number of salmon in the Shannon was very much depleted compared to a generation before, but from my perspective, growing up there as a child, there still seemed to be enough to go around.

Despite much attention being paid to poaching, by far the biggest threat to the Atlantic wild salmon in the Shannon was the Ardnacrusha power station, that jewel in the crown of independent Ireland. While many people found employment in its construction, and the whole country benefitted from the power it generated, it wreaked absolute havoc on the salmon population from the very start.

This issue is my lifelong obsession. I am horrified and aghast that successive governments have overlooked the devastation of our rivers and all that they contain. We know so much more about biodiversity and the environment now than we did back in the 1920s and '30s, when Ireland was working so hard to become a modern nation and yet, for some reason, we seem collectively incapable of coming together to save even one of the keystone species of our beautiful island.

Why does it matter? You need to know a little about these incredible creatures to understand.

* * *

Salmon are adventurers, brave and noble wanderers. They travel the world, yet never forget where they come from. They are also, of course, extremely delicious and nutritious, which is why the exploitation of salmon by people is as old as human habitation wherever they are found.

Atlantic salmon are found all over the North Atlantic Ocean and in the freshwater rivers that flow into it. In the twenty-first century, we are used to thinking of salmon as a food item, and to seeing it chopped into ready-to-cook pieces, carefully wrapped in plastic, on the shelves of supermarket chilled cabinets. We have largely forgotten that salmon are also extraordinarily beautiful creatures. They have slender, graceful bodies with elegant heads. They are a silvery colour, tending to white on their undersides, and their upper skin is marked with blueish-green spots. A healthy salmon is a joy to behold.

Atlantic salmon are a migratory species, which need a different habitat for each period of their life cycle. They have an anadromous life cycle, meaning that they are born in rivers, spend most of their lives in saltwater, and return to their natal river to spawn in freshwater.

Despite the toughness and resilience they display in their challenging journey through life, Atlantic salmon require a very particular environment in order to successfully reproduce. They need fresh water that is clear and cold, and that moves quickly over a gravelly surface, with rocky outcrops that serve as nurseries for young fish.

Left to their own devices, salmon will invariably choose to spawn in their own natal river. The journey from the Atlantic to their spawning grounds is exhausting, as they stop eating to doggedly pursue their goal. They may travel for thousands of kilometres to return to where they came from, guided by instinct and a keen sense of smell. When they reach fresh water, their colour changes from a silvery hue to a browner colour, a better camouflage in river water. Now, they must swim upstream, against the current, until they reach their spawning grounds.

After spawning for the first time, the salmon may return to the ocean, where it will eat and regain strength. It may return to spawn for a second time, but many will spawn only once, and hardly any more than twice.

Large numbers die from exhaustion at the end of their journey home.

Each river, and each of its tributaries, has its own unique chemical composition, and by means that are still imperfectly understood, the salmon guide themselves back to where they came from. Salmon have a sense of smell estimated to be a thousand times greater than that of a dog, and it is thought that they use this to find their way home.[46] About 2,500 salmon rivers flow into the North Atlantic[47] and yet, left to their own devices, the salmon all remember their own, and know how to return to it.

Once she has reached her native river, the female – known as a 'hen' – carefully chooses a suitable area of the river, where there is a constant flow of water and very little variation in depth or temperature. When she is satisfied that she has found a good spot, she digs a nest in the gravel, known as a 'redd'. This is very hard work for the hen, who has to roll onto her side and use her tail muscles to excavate the gravel, dislodging small stones that can then roll away in the river current. Periodically, as the redd gets deeper, she checks its depth by lowering herself into the nest.

Only after all this challenging work has been completed does the male get involved. Several males – known as 'cocks' – may approach the redd-building hen, and a number of them may fight for access to her and engage in courtship rituals to impress her, like quivering and swimming over her back. If the hen dislikes a particular male, she will move away from him to make her point clear; if she likes him, she will allow him to approach.

When she is ready to lay her eggs, the hen lowers herself into the redd, and the cock moves in beside her. As her eggs, orange-red in colour, leave her body and settle into the gaps between the stones in the redd, his semen – known as milt – leaves his body and lands on the eggs, fertilising them. Both salmon must deposit their gametes at the same time, as the unfertilised eggs will only survive outside the mother's body for about a minute and a half.[48] Salmon mothers produce prodigious quantities of eggs, from about 450 to 750 per pound of her body weight.

Sometimes, at the last minute, an unsuccessful male may manage to dart in and deposit some of his own milt in an effort to ensure the transmission of his genes. The female may build another redd, depending on how much energy she has left, and she may remain in the area to defend her eggs for a period of time.

After spawning, salmon are known as 'kelts'. Younger, more vigorous kelts may return to the ocean to repeat the cycle again, but many die of exhaustion after spawning. Hardly any survive more than three reproductive cycles.

The salmon eggs remain under the gravel all winter, slowly developing. From an early developmental stage, you can tell at a glance which eggs have been successfully fertilised, because they are translucent and the developing embryos inside can be clearly seen. They initially look like a little dark dot, and they are known as 'eyed ova' during these initial stages of development. After about three months, in early spring, they hatch from the soft shells of the eggs. At this stage, they are known as 'alevins'. At first, alevins barely resemble fish at all, except for their eyes, which are relatively large and appear well-developed compared to the rest of them. They retain a sac of egg yolk, which hangs on their undersides as a nutrient-rich food supply that their bodies absorb gradually until they become capable of independent foraging.

By this stage, the baby salmon have become fry, and can swim and eat by themselves, so they start to leave the redd. They are now clearly fish, but are still very small, and only those with a very good knowledge of salmon would be able to identify them from other species. They are not strong enough to swim against the current, so they are carried by the fast-flowing water until they find themselves in a quiet area with pools, where the calmer water permits them to remain in one place, and their camouflage helps to hide them. Sometimes they are found in large numbers in these environments, living on a diet of the larvae of insects like mayflies, plankton and other fish eggs. In this aquatic nursery they can stay and grow. After about a year, those that have survived the fry stage are from five to eight centimetres long and have developed camouflage markers – stripes along their backs and sides that mimic shadows on the water and help protect them from predators. Now they are known as 'parr'. They remain in freshwater streams and rivers, eating and slowly growing. This process of physiological, morphological and behavioural change is known as 'smoltification'.

The parr now develop into smolts – young salmon with a silver colouring and dark fins. In the Shannon, this process usually takes between a year and three years. Smolts consume flies and other insects and increasingly also other forms of aquatic life, occasionally including smaller fish. Fishing people who know a particular stretch of water very well can often identify smolts from specific tributaries – the markings on their skin can vary slightly, depending on where they were born and the sort of camouflage that serves them well there.

When the smolts are ready to move on from their native river, their bodies undergo a chemical shift to balance their salt levels and, like countless generations of their ancestors, they migrate downstream to the Atlantic. In the Atlantic, they will spend between one and three years travelling, eating a diet including krill, plankton and small fish. They grow and accumulate substantial amounts of body fat. These fat deposits, which make them so delectable, will sustain them during their demanding reproductive cycle.

As adults, salmon can be quite a solitary species. The Atlantic is enormous, so salmon might rarely ever encounter one another. They may come together only when congregating in their feeding grounds – notably in the icy waters off Greenland, to which millions of salmon travel to feed – and when returning to their native rivers. Divers along the Atlantic coast have observed salmon swimming together in schools, and it appears that different salmon populations, from diverse rivers and tributaries, can recognise one another as they congregate with their peers.

At all stages of the salmon's life cycle, multiple predators consume them. Fish of all sorts might find a redd, open it and eat all the eggs, while bigger fish – including bigger salmon – eat the smaller ones, and water-based or water-adjacent mammals such as mink, riverside rats and otters all join in the feast. At sea, they are consumed by large fish like Atlantic halibut, bluefin tuna, swordfish and striped bass; as well as by sharks, by seabirds like gannets, and by seals. This, of course, is just nature feeding itself, as it does, and is all perfectly normal and natural. Given these high rates of attrition, the number of adult salmon that reach the age to spawn is a minuscule percentage of the number that manage to hatch from their mother's eggs, which are already a small percentage of the number of eggs laid in the first place.

Regardless of whether they manage to spawn just once or several times in a lifetime, a salmon can travel many thousands of kilometres and, presumably, see many wonderful things. Every salmon that makes it to adulthood is a conquering hero that has already beaten enormous odds. Their adventurous and challenging lives – their heroes' journeys – have been inspiring artists and storytellers for literally thousands of years.

Salmon fishermen have a special vocabulary for discussing the fish. In Ireland, the ones that return to their native rivers in early spring or even in the winter are known as 'spring fish'. They are further subdivided by size, depending on how many years they have spent feeding in the Atlantic. Those that return in the summer are known as 'grilse', 'peal' or 'summer fish', again divided by size depending on how long they have spent in the ocean.[49] Each area that catches salmon also has a unique local vocabulary for the minute details of the fish and their environment. I grew up with a detailed knowledge of this vocabulary in the Shannon Estuary area and still sometimes forget that not everybody shares it.

* * *

Ordinary fishing people, like the many families at Coonagh who depended heavily on the Shannon for their livelihoods, may not have realised at first the impact the Shannon Scheme would have on the fisheries, but engineers and scientists had some idea from the start. Some measures were taken that were supposed to mitigate it. Even before the construction of Ardnacrusha power station began, local authorities had noted the need for a 'fish ladder' at the weir.

A fish pass measuring 190 metres, consisting of thirteen steps and carrying a tiny percentage of the Shannon water, was installed at Parteen Weir in the hope that it would allow fish, particularly migrating salmon, to make their way upstream. A fish, however, will naturally assume that the best way forward is to aim for the biggest volume of water, so inevitably the pass – with very little water – was difficult for the fish to find, and many never did.

It was also predicted that many fish would try to move upstream at the site of the Ardnacrusha power station, and various proposals to make things easier for them were considered. Engineers even discussed building a hydraulic fish lift, but the technology of the time was not up to the challenge. It was finally decided to use the navigation locks as a fish lift, but because salmon moving upstream do not like to swim into still water, this was not successful. More success was had in helping smolts to move downstream,[50] but unless adults could get upstream to spawn, the number of smolts was inevitably going to decline year on year.

Rather cynically, the authorities exploited a legal loophole. Under nineteenth-century legislation known as the 'Queen's Gap Act', provision had to be made for the passage of fish across dams and weirs built on all natural rivers and watercourses. However, the Ardnacrusha dam was constructed on a canal, an artificial watercourse, and was therefore deemed exempt from the legal requirement for a fish pass.[51] Technically speaking, the construction of this artificial watercourse was, in itself, a breach of the law by the authorities. As electrification was so important, however, the need for a power station was deemed more urgent than the need to protect the environment.

It appears that at the time of the construction of Ardnacrusha power station, when local fishing communities were very anxious about what the changes would mean for them, it was known for bailiffs to arm themselves with serious weapons, including revolvers, and terrorise the locals.[52] There seems to have been a long history in the area of bailiffs double-jobbing as fishermen while also patrolling the fishing of others.[53]

Minutes of a meeting held on 16 February 1927 referred to a prior event when employees of a private company, the Lax Weir Company, intimidated the local fishermen.[54] In 1925, Shannon bailiffs had been patrolling the water in a motorboat owned by the Lax Weir Company when they came across about twenty boats, each crewed by three Coonagh men – many of whom I knew in their later years, when I was a child. The fishermen attacked the bailiffs with their oars, while a supporting crowd composed of their wives and children yelled and threw stones from the riverbank.[55]

Apparently, a similar event had taken place in Coonagh in 1926, when some bailiffs themselves attempted fishing in waters used by Coonagh fishermen, and were allegedly assaulted by some local women defending their families' fishing grounds.[56] The bailiffs would prevent locals from fishing in a particular spot, so to see them helping themselves pushed the fishing families over the edge.

When I was growing up, Mam related an account of this event from the locals' point of view. She remembered that the bailiffs had approached the riverbank and attacked local fishermen in the muddy area between the river and the land. Their wives – Mam mentioned a neighbour-woman called McInerny, whose family was still in the area when I was a child – leapt to their husbands' defence. Mrs McInenry apparently practically flattened one of the bailiffs and sent him off with his tail between his legs. The whole affair was remembered locally as the Battle of the Pool. Two years later, Anthony Mackey, in the Minute Book of Limerick No. 8 Fishery District, recorded that bailiffs employed by the Lax Weir company, armed with expensive revolvers, were continuing to 'terrorise' working fishermen in the area.[57]

Before 1928, the spawning beds below Parteen Weir had been the most important in the entire Shannon. At that time, the channel was wide and there was a plentiful flow of water when the salmon were spawning. After the construction of Ardnacrusha power station, there was a significant reduction in the amount of water flowing down the old channel, because now most of the Shannon water was diverted for generating electricity. Now, portions of what had previously been the riverbed were actually dry for part or all of the spawning season. Some salmon continued to lay their eggs in this area, but many of them dried out and died when the water level fell, dramatically reducing numbers in the next generation of fish.[58] Other salmon tried to reach parts of the riverbed upstream from the station, but died of exhaustion before they were able to reproduce.

The hydroelectric plant had been hailed as one of the new State's crowning achievements – which it was – but for the river fish, especially the salmon, it was a disaster. The traditional fishing grounds of the area had already been severely impacted. Some were now completely off-limits to fishing communities that had worked them for generations, and others were already seeing severe reductions in the numbers of fish. With each year that passed, their numbers continued to drop.

The slightest change in climatic conditions had an outsized impact on the hugely altered river. When there was a dry spell, extra water from the river channel was diverted to serve the hydropower station, reducing the flow of water even more. In January 1931, the water in the original river channel was so low that it was at normal summer levels, at the time when the salmon needed to reach their spawning grounds. Locals saw salmon swimming about in a state of agitation. The same thing happened the next year, in February, and the Limerick Fisheries Board wrote to the ESB, asking for water to be diverted down the old riverbed to allow the salmon to pass. The request was denied, because the power station needed all the water it could get during the dry spell. The spawning grounds were consequently left only partially covered with water, leaving the eggs vulnerable to destruction from frost and birds. Problems of this nature with the spawning grounds continued throughout the 1930s,[59] but it was considered cheaper to pay the fishing families off than to address the issue in a more meaningful way.

In 1925, 1933, 1934 and 1935, the Shannon Electricity Acts, and various amendments, outlined who was eligible for compensation for damage to their livelihood resulting from the Shannon Scheme. Among these were many of the Shannon fishermen.[60] Some fishing families, angry and desperate about the dramatic drop in their incomes, were said locally to have deliberately destroyed some of the embankments that prevented flooding, in the hope of being hired by the council to repair them. Newspaper reports at the time refer to stones being displaced in retaining walls.[61] The rather verbose wording of the Act also grants hydroelectricity the right to override the needs of the fish, which are offered protection only if this does not cause 'substantial detriment to the works or substantial hindrance to their construction'.[62] In other words, the needs of electrical production were to predominate over all other interests.

A new government, under de Valera, had been elected in March 1932. De Valera represented the constituency of Clare, and as many of those negatively affected by the Shannon Scheme lived in Clare, they were hopeful that he might try to help. Moreover, many of the fishermen were republicans who had taken de Valera's side during the recent Civil War.[63]

Meanwhile, the Abbey Guild of Fishermen were increasingly angry. A collective of fishing families with a long history in the area, they traditionally fished the waters between Limerick City and the area of Doonass with short snap nets (up to twenty yards long, hung from a thin top rope, with stones at either end of the net on the bottom rope, stretched between two boats). Since the construction of Ardnacrusha power station, their livelihoods had been decimated. By the early 1930s, about sixty-four men were working full-time on the Abbey Guild's fisheries during the fishing season. They would pick up casual work in the bacon and construction industries – both very big employers in Limerick – at other times of the year, while the women were involved in processing and selling fish.[64] Fishing was prohibited in the tail race of the power station, where fish were dying in their thousands. The few fish that had managed to find their way upstream generally remained blocked above it when they attempted to make their way back, or were churned into fishmeal by the relentless turbines.[65]

On the night of 11 July 1932, the Abbey fishermen moved twenty-four boats into the tail race and dropped their nets in protest, even as representatives from the Fisheries Board yelled from the banks that what they were doing was against the law.[66] By 13 July, the fishermen were being pursued on the water by motor launches of bailiffs and civic guards, and revolvers were shot into the air.[67] Hundreds of onlookers lined the banks, watching to see how events would unfold. The crowds were sympathetic to the fishermen, who had been assured at the start of the Shannon Scheme that their fishing rights would be respected.[68] But rights to fish were all but meaningless when there were almost no fish to be caught.

The fishermen continued their protest over the subsequent three nights, until all of their nets and boats had been confiscated, the boats being transported and held at Sarsfield Barracks in the city.[69] There were many complaints about police brutality meted out to the protestors.

On 18 July, the fishermen's boats and nets were returned to them, and later, charges of illegal fishing against them were dropped. But nothing changed the situation at hand, which was that they were now cut off from the fish that had previously provided them with their livelihoods.

The struggles of the Abbey Fishermen were particularly intense, but fishing communities elsewhere on the Shannon were in much the same situation. The Shannon Scheme had generated huge goodwill during its construction and was still a major local employer as works were ongoing, but the relationship between the State and local fishing communities was increasingly oppositional. Many fishing families now seemed to have to choose between fighting a battle they would never win or leaving an area where they had lived and worked for generations.

In 1934, a Shannon Fisheries Act stated that henceforth no licences would be issued to fish with a snap net in the tidal waters of the Shannon.[70] In 1935, ownership of the Lax Weir, which dated back to Viking times, was transferred to the ESB. Further Shannon Fisheries Acts in the 1930s gave the ESB all the freshwater fishing rights in the Shannon and the commercial fishing rights in the Shannon Estuary,[71] with compensation paid to the previous holders of these rights. Of course, the ESB would not make the health of the fisheries a priority, as its primary role was to ensure the constant provision of electricity. The loss of fish, and the impact on fishermen's livelihoods, was inevitable. By 1936, the Abbey fishermen had no choice but to accept compensation for the loss of their livelihood, and they disappeared from the Shannon.[72]

Around this time, there was also an increase in river fatalities. The new hydroelectric plant had massively impacted on the way the Shannon waters ran through the landscape. Used to working on the water, but unfamiliar with the incredible speeds and rapid changes of the artificially diverted water, various fatalities in the early years of operation were directly related to the topographical changes.

As Mam and Dad celebrated the birth of their first child, baby Margaret, and settled into their married lives in Coonagh, the measures taken to protect the salmon were steadily seen to fail. By now, the declining stock of salmon was very evident, and commercial fishing of salmon declined dramatically. The government had made it clear that, when there was a clash of interests, the electricity works were considered more important than the fisheries.[73] The writing was on the wall.

By the academic year of 1937/8, schoolchildren from Coonagh whose fathers used drift nets – much larger than the snap nets of the Abbey fishermen – reported the restrictions placed on their dads' fishing activities. It had always been the case that they could fish only on particular days and in specific parts of the river,[74] but now fish numbers were so reduced that it was increasingly difficult for them to make a viable income during those restricted times. Already, there were perceptibly fewer fish than before – the supply so small since the Shannon Scheme, one child reported, that many fishing families were simply giving up.[75]

By the time I was born on 21 May 1943, things had already changed considerably for the fishermen of Coonagh. Increasingly, the men from the community worked for the council in road construction, or in jobs in Limerick City, rather than fishing.[76] That might not sound like such a terrible thing, but these men had been self-employed entrepreneurs, with livelihoods that depended on an intimate knowledge of the local ecology. Doing monotonous work for the county council, having to observe a hierarchy of authority and being told when to start and finish work could be hard. Even when the pay wasn't too bad, it seemed to erode their very sense of identity.

All around the North Atlantic, salmon were facing the same challenges. Across northwestern Europe, and in the United States and Canada, hydroelectric plants were being built across major salmon rivers. For the first time, countless industries were able to mechanise, and innumerable homes were lit up with electricity. And in all of those rivers – every single one – the numbers of Atlantic salmon, and of other species too, started to drop, for all the same reasons as in Ireland.

Since time immemorial, fishermen – the hunters of the sea and of our rivers and lakes – have made it their life's work to understand the salmon's journey. In Ireland alone, a large number of technologies, from the primitive to the cutting-edge, have been used over the centuries for catching salmon.[77] It seems there is almost nothing we will not collectively do to satisfy our hunger for salmon, even if it means hunting them to extinction. At the same time, the constant pressures of modernisation and progress have meant that governments the world over have sacrificed the well-being of wild species to generate power. The challenges facing traditional salmon-fishing communities, and the salmon, have continued to mount.

How did we get into this situation?

And how can we get out of it?

Finding the answers to these questions is, quite literally, the story of my life.

CHAPTER TWO

A River Childhood

The details of the origins of the Peril family are lost to the mists of time, but one theory is that they came to Ireland with the Normans, and settled in the west. At one stage, there were quite a few living on the now-depopulated Island Eddy in Galway Bay. Historical records show our ancestors, who spelled their name 'Perrell' and 'Parell' in the 1500s,[78] as having been associated with the castle on the island. By the time Dad – Patrick Peril – was born in about 1910, his family was living in the Gaeltacht area of Inchaboy, near Gort in Galway. Their surname is recorded as 'Perrill' in the census.

Dad's family – his parents were Michael and Kate – were farmers then, which in the days before modern agricultural technology was one of the most difficult ways to make a living, especially on the rough, thin, rocky soil of that part of Galway. In the 1911 census, the family was recorded as speaking Irish and English, but it is likely that Dad's parents did not speak English very well. Dad himself, having attended national school, was perfectly bilingual. He retained good Irish all his life, and there were certain phrases that he would routinely say in Irish: '*ná déan é sin*' – 'don't do that' – is one I remember him saying often. The Gort area was noted for hurling, and several of the family were strong hurlers, who were even said to have played in finals in Croke Park in the 1880s, shortly after the GAA was founded.

Although they lived inland, the Perils weren't too far from the coastal village of Kinvarra. Dad and his siblings often went there to visit friends and play cards, and I believe this is where Dad picked up the boating and fishing skills that would be so central to his way of life, and that he would pass down to me. The family also had some involvement with the turf boats that transported turf up and down the west coast. This may have put them in touch with people in the Limerick area, where turf boats transported the fuel up and down the Shannon Estuary area.[79]

I know that Dad's family had strongly republican views, but I do not know much about what they experienced during the turbulent early years of the twentieth century. History books recount some of the stories of the War of Independence and the Civil War, but naturally they leave a lot of them out too. Both wars had a massive impact on rural families and communities all over Ireland. Dad was very young at the time, but he still had his stories to tell. His home area was deeply republican and the people there had suffered terribly during the era of the Black and Tans – the British forces sent over from 1920 to put down the uprising, with intimidation, violence and reprisals. Dad was always very vague on the issue of what, if anything, his family members did during the War of Independence, but from the hints he dropped, it was clear that they had some involvement in the local hostilities.

After independence, the Civil War raged fiercely in his home area too. Dad actually saw a man being shot dead by others who had once been his friends. He would never forget it. Views varied among the siblings in Dad's family regarding who was right and who was wrong in the Civil War, but I believe they managed to hold opposing views and not fall out about them, which was quite an achievement in those tense days. Dad remained proudly and unwaveringly nationalist all his life.

Mam was Honora Foley, known as Nora. Mam grew up in the parish of Parteen, a mile or two downstream from Parteen Weir. She was the daughter of Tom Foley from Crecora in Limerick, who also worked with the land, and was descended on her mother's side from the Kennys of Coonagh, a village a few miles from Parteen, who were salmon fishermen, seafaring people and farmers. Tom had a reputation for being a great ploughman and was in much demand locally for this skilled and important work. Mam also had stories to tell about the War of Independence in the area around Parteen and Coonagh.

Many IRA men had managed to flee pursuers by using local knowledge to cross the Shannon Estuary quickly and safely. On one occasion, a British Brigadier General, Cuthbert Lucas, was held captive by a local IRA unit, transported across the Shannon and deposited in a nearby house for safe keeping; Lucas had been captured in Cork on 26 June 1920, while engaging in salmon fishing on the River Blackwater. His captors treated him well and gave him whatever he wanted – he was even taken out for a bit of recreational salmon-poaching on the river. Probably out of sheer boredom, he requested a bottle of whiskey every day, and drank them all. Apparently he also partook with enthusiasm in games of poker, and generally won. Eventually, although the IRA lads had grown fond of him and regarded him as a sort of pet, Cuthbert was getting too expensive to keep, and they let him escape. Afterwards, he wrote a letter thanking the IRA for how he had been treated, and described the IRA boys as 'delightful' and as 'gentlemen.'

But Mam also remembered the brutality of those strange days. She recalled the Black and Tans coming into the village of Coonagh in the middle of the day. They threatened to shoot a number of teenage boys hunkered down behind a stone wall, until the local shopkeeper – a Mrs O'Halloran – intervened, saying that they were just kids at play and did not deserve to be killed.

Coonagh had already suffered terribly during the First World War, with huge losses among the young men who had signed up to fight – eight died on 13 May 1915, when the British HMS *Goliath* was sunk in the Dardanelles, giving Coonagh a strikingly high death toll per head of population. More died during the Spanish Flu; I imagine the thought of the Black and Tans further decimating the already suffering community was too much to bear and gave Mrs O'Halloran the courage she needed to confront them. She was just lucky, I suppose, that they didn't turn their weapons on her, or perhaps she managed to prick a conscience or two.

Like most girls in the area then, Mam left school young. She worked as a domestic servant for a wealthy local business family called Holmes, and then in the garda station on William Street in Limerick City, meaning that she got to see at first hand the development of policing in a still very young independent Ireland. She cleaned the station and kept the gardaí fed and watered. Mam was never afraid of hard work.

The Shannon Scheme brought my parents together, so without it I would never have been born. One of the thousands of strong, young men employed in the building of the Ardnacrusha project was Dad, one of the aforementioned tough guys from Galway. When the labouring jobs were advertised, Dad got on his bike and cycled all the way from Galway to Limerick; he was a strong cyclist all his life.

They were lucky to have him, because Dad was also a very hard worker. He must still have been in his teens when he started at Ardnacrusha, and having known him later on, I am sure he gave the work his all. I think Dad probably pretended to be several years older than he really was to get the work. In those days, it was common for young lads to leave school at twelve or thirteen and pass themselves off as sixteen or seventeen if they could get away with it, just to get a job. Dad was always proud to have played a part in the Shannon Scheme, which was such a crucial step towards fiscal autonomy for the newly independent Ireland that so many had fought so hard for. He was one of those who stayed on after the station opened in 1929, and was still working on the expanding infrastructure in the 1930s.

Although the work on the Shannon Scheme was extremely demanding, Dad's memories of it were generally positive. In particular, he spoke very highly of the German engineers, foremen and labourers, whom he regarded as hard-working, thorough and fair-minded men. Dad's memories of working with the Germans gave me an interest in them too, and I have been fascinated with German engineering, and German culture generally, all my life.

Dad often recounted the sad story of one of the German supervisors, Jacob Kuntz, who was known to keep his wages and savings on his person, sewn into the lining of his clothes. Jacob was waylaid and attacked on the railway line near the village of Parteen on 21 December 1928. He was found alive, covered in blood, and brought straight to St John's Hospital in Limerick, where he died shortly after. Two days later, a man called John Cox, a veteran of the First World War who was also employed on the Shannon Scheme, was arrested for Jacob's murder.[80]

On 11 March 1929, Cox was found guilty of murder, with a recommendation for clemency from the jury. He was executed by hanging, which was carried out by a professional English hangman, Pierrepoint, at Mountjoy Prison on 25 April of the same year. John's last words were, 'Well, here I go, boys. I will pray for you all when I go above.'[81] The local newspapers covered the whole awful case for weeks, and the local community would talk about it for years – they were still talking about it in the 1940s and '50s, when I was growing up nearby. Jacob had been a well-liked man, and the Cox family had been respected locally too. It was all just dreadful. In a small community, a violent incident like that can have a ripple effect that lasts for generations.

At some point in the early 1930s, Mam and Dad met and fell in love. In those days, the big thing was to have house dances. Any house with a substantial floor was suitable, and the young people would dance to céilí and other types of music all night long, stopping only when the sun started to appear over the horizon. I think it was at one of these dances that Mam and Dad first set eyes on one another. He had lodgings nearby, so they arranged to see each other again, and they started to court.

By the mid-1930s, houses and businesses all over the country were lighting up with electricity provided by the thundering turbines at Ardnacrusha. Animosities relating to the War of Independence and the Civil War had started to abate somewhat, but Dad remained deeply interested in the nationalist cause post-independence, after starting to put down roots in the Limerick area. He was involved in some capacity with an IRA brigade. He would serve nine months in Arbour Hill Prison in Dublin – where many IRA men were held – between 1936 and 1937, and was released on parole during that time for just long enough to marry Mam, who was expecting their first child.

The records on him that are still held at the National Military Archive are brief and matter-of-fact, but surprisingly moving. They include the reassuring detail that neither Dad nor anyone in his family showed any sign of insanity; a letter from Mam requesting permission to visit Dad in prison, along with her father; and the documentation relating to Dad's temporary release shortly afterwards, so that he could participate in what the authorities delicately referred to as a 'necessary marriage'.

It must have been a very stressful time for Mam, as Ireland was tough on unmarried mothers in those days, and she would have been anxious to get married as soon as possible. She was working at the police station in Limerick at the time, and it appears that her employer helped her to get Dad out of prison for just long enough to 'make an honest woman' of her. I knew very little of this when I was growing up – just the fact that Dad had served some time in detention for his nationalist activities. Needless to say, Mam and Dad never talked about the fact that their first child had been conceived before they were married.

It is lovely – heart-warming, really – to see that, even in those harsh days, the military and police personnel involved with them both were compassionate, and went out of their way to support a young couple starting out in life. If Dad had not been allowed out for that 'necessary marriage', both of their lives could have turned out very differently.

Mam and Dad set up home initially in Mam's home area of Parteen, later moving to the tiny fishing community of Coonagh, on the outskirts of Limerick City, just on the Limerick/Clare border. Their home was a small, reed-thatched building, one of the oldest in the village – said locally to date to the time of the Vikings. It was almost within a stone's throw of the heavy flow of the Shannon, to the side of the local 'fairy fort', which may well have been the remains of a fortified dwelling dating back to the Iron Age. Just across a field stood the remains of a brickworks that had been a major source of local employment until the late nineteenth century because bricks from Coonagh were used to build Limerick.

Dad was no longer involved with Ardnacrusha now, but he was still contributing to the modernisation of Ireland: the cement factory where he worked provided raw materials for the significant levels of building – housing, industrial buildings, hospitals and other institutions – that were then underway.

At the same time, he was also deeply involved in keeping tradition alive. Although Dad's parents had been farming people, his family had always maintained a connection with the sea and he had long known how to handle a boat. He was also now connected through marriage to a well-known local fishing family, and had access to the rich fishing grounds of the Shannon river and estuary in Coonagh, where he and Mam had set up home. He used traditional tools and techniques to catch fish and also to harvest the reeds that grew thickly along the banks of the Shannon. Fishing was by no means an easy job, and everyone in Coonagh had to work extremely hard to make ends meet, but the Shannon was still rich in salmon, relative to today, and the market for the delicious wild fish was great.

The Ardnacrusha power station was powering a steadily growing number of industries around the country. The government was meanwhile opening further power stations of various kinds, and eventually there would also be hydroelectrical stations on the Lee, the Erne and the Liffey.[82] I think that people of my parents' generation were hopeful that their children's futures would be much brighter than theirs had been.

* * *

The first thing I can remember, from when I was about three or four years old, is the sound of small aeroplanes. I can remember as if it was yesterday the rumble of their engines and how I ran, stumbling over my feet, from inside our little house in my home village of Coonagh, just a few miles from the heart of bustling Limerick City, on the shores of the great River Shannon. Watching them pass by overhead was the start of my lifelong passion for aviation.

Although I didn't realise it at the time, those little planes were also a powerful symbol for the Ireland of those days. We were then one of the poorest countries in western Europe, struggling to embrace modernisation, no matter what. Countless communities like mine were still without electricity, running water or sanitation.

I was one of eight children in the Peril family, of whom seven survived. In order of birth, we survivors were Michael, Kathleen, Tom, me, Johnny, Tony and Mary. Mam and Dad's first child, Margaret, had died as a baby – the teenage girl who was holding her accidentally dropped her, and she hit her head in just the wrong place. While Mam and Dad never talked much about little Margaret, at some point they had removed her tin grave-marker from her burial place and put it on a shelf in our one-roomed house. I used to lie in bed and look at it in the flicker of the lamplight, going over in my mind what I had overheard the grown-ups saying about Margaret's short life and tragic death. She had, they said, been a beautiful child. Too good for this Earth. Sometimes someone would say that Mam and Dad should take her grave-marker down from the shelf, that it was not doing either of them any good to dwell on the past when they had a fine, healthy family to rear and be proud of. Listening to the sad story of baby Margaret is how I learned about death, and the reality of my own – and everyone else's – mortality. At just four years of age or so, I started to worry that I might die too, and would fall asleep with this thought in my mind.

Mam and Dad were both very hard-working people, and all through my childhood they laboured diligently to keep us all warmly clothed, with plenty of food on the table for the growing family. Dad had a labouring job in the local cement factory – a Danish-owned company and a major local employer – and during the fishing season he would also put in a second shift fishing for salmon on the river. He liked a drink and often came home a little the worse for wear in the evenings, having stopped for a pint or three of Guinness on the way. He was never, however, late for work, and he had a very good rep-utation locally as a diligent, hard worker. His stocky frame and strong arms and shoulders were proof of the tough, physical effort that was his speciality.

Mam had her hands extremely full taking care of the house and the children, along with whatever paid work she could pick up locally. During busy times on local farms, the bigger farmers drove around in lorries to communities like Coonagh, picking up women who were available for casual work. Some of the farms were attached to institutions such as hospitals or religious orders. I remember Mam and a few other women from the village lining up on the side of the road to wait, and then pulling themselves up into the back of a vehicle, joining other women labourers who had already been collected at various points along the route.

A typical day for Mam involved getting up early to give everyone their breakfast, and then spending the entire day bent over in a field, weeding carrot or turnip drills, for which she was paid a pittance. She was also an expert milker, and was hired by local farmers to milk their cows. This meant rising at four in the morning and walking across the fields to where the cattle were at pasture; she milked them in the open air into a bucket. I can remember seeing the silver coins – never paper money, because she did not earn enough for that – being counted out into her hand. After a hard day's work in a field, she came home and had to make the evening meal for the whole family, or had to wash our clothes in a tin basin with a washboard and a tablet of soap.

Looking back now, I can see that our way of life was not easy, even by the standards of the 1940s and '50s. But I can honestly say that I never felt poor as a child, because there was always healthy food on the table, at a time when plenty of families in Ireland were going to bed with empty bellies. Our family home, and the fishing community of Coonagh in general, was a loving, nurturing environment in which to grow up.

Dad's salary from the cement factory, and the money he made fishing, paid for the family's basic needs (including the tobacco that most adults were addicted to in those days). The many hours that Mam spent weeding in other people's fields – starting as early as four or five in the morning on summer days – paid for the extras, such as our Holy Communion and Confirmation outfits. There were no utility bills to pay then, because we had no utilities.

Despite being just down the road from Ardnacrusha, one of Europe's most impressive and modern power stations, there was no electric light in Coonagh until the mid-1950s. Instead, our homes were illuminated by the flicker of paraffin oil lamps. It is funny: although my dad and many others had worked on the Shannon Scheme themselves not long before, I do not remember any bitterness in Coonagh about the fact that the electricity had not reached us yet. In fact, we kids loved filling the two oil lamps that we used to light our home, and my siblings and I squabbled on a daily basis about whose turn it was to do it.

By that time, most rural communities had been given water pumps by the State, with each pump shared by a number of families. We had a pump on the side of the road in Coonagh, but in the main we preferred to use one of the six local wells located on the floodplain, where the Shannon River met the land. The water there was fresh, clean and delicious, so long as nobody tampered with it. When someone came to the house and was offered a glass of water, they would often say, 'Where did you get it?' When we answered, 'From the Bawneen Well!', they would drink up with satisfaction, because they knew it was good. There were plenty of stories about local farmers, landowners wealthier than most of the residents of Coonagh, who deliberately contaminated the water in wells on their land, because they did not want people walking across their fields to access it.

Our house was one of three in a small terrace, constructed with thick stone walls plastered on the inside only. The lower part outside was tarpainted to prevent rising damp, and freshly whitewashed most years above the line of the tar. The roof was thatched with Shannon reeds that Dad himself harvested along the riverbanks just metres away. Dad was a very competent thatcher. When I was old enough, I would go up on the roof with Dad, helping him to place the bundles of thatch and secure them. We had two four-paned windows, both to the front of the house, and a heavy, green-painted wooden door with a latch that we rarely, if ever, locked. This was partly because we had nothing to steal, but mostly because we knew and trusted all our neighbours, who were like family to us.

We were a close-knit family in many ways. For one thing, nobody had any secrets from anyone else, as we all lived in one room, portioned off into sections to provide some privacy, with flowered curtains strung from wall to wall on wooden rails. I slept in a big bed with my brothers, all of us together in a tangle of arms and legs, while Mam and Dad and the newest baby slept on the other side. The living area had a big table and Mam's lovely dresser, crammed with the beautiful coloured delph that was her pride and joy.

Beyond the family, the whole community was very close, and all of our lives were intimately intertwined. In the daytime and in the evenings, friends and neighbours of Mam and Dad often dropped by, and we children would earwig on their conversations, hearing the bits of news and gossip that were passed around the village. When someone was born, when someone was sick or when someone died, these were all occasions for neighbours to come together and support one another as best they could. We had regular channels of communication with Dad's side of the family, above in Galway, and my sister Kathleen was actually raised by our grandparents there for a few years. She was absolutely doted on, and I imagine it was tough enough for her coming back and having to compete for attention with all her brothers while we laughed at her Galway accent.

Mam was also very close to her own siblings, John and Mary. Mary had married a man called Christy Keegan from Parteen village. The Keegans were a well-known local family, deeply embedded in the community there. Their dead were buried in Kilquane Cemetery, a small green graveyard on the banks of the Shannon, a hundred yards from the Lax Weir and opposite St Thomas's Island, where it was said there once was a monastery. A sibling of Mam's was buried there too, in the grave of one of the Kellys, another local family. In those days, infant mortality was so high that babies who died were often buried in the most convenient grave, rather than necessarily in their family plot.

Mam's people and the Keegans and Kellys alike were steeped in the lore and history of the place they came from. She and her relatives told stories said to date back to the time of the Danes – a bold but not impossible claim, as the Lax Weir at Parteen was originally built by the Vikings. It still bore the name they gave it – 'lax' means 'salmon' in their language and the word 'lax' is found in placenames everywhere the Vikings settled.

I would often come home from school to find two of Mam's uncles there, my great-uncles The Yank and Old Drag (a lot of people went by their nicknames in those days; I know The Yank had spent some time in America, and Old Drag may have earned his nickname digging dykes or fishing with a net). They would be sitting one on either side of the fire in the dark clothes that all the men wore in those days, watching the flames and chatting about the local news, or even singing.

Our diet, which would otherwise have been very basic, was regularly supplemented with delicious salmon and other fish that Dad had caught. There would sometimes be game, such as rabbit, or wild mallard or plover (I can still hear Mam grumbling as she laboriously picked the lead shot out of the meat before roasting or boiling it). In those days, rabbits were everywhere, and you would often meet a man on his way back from a rabbit hunt with maybe twenty of them dangling from his bicycle handlebars, and more hanging across his shoulders or even from his hat.

We also had fresh eggs from the five or six hens that Mam kept in a coop outside in our large front garden. We children were responsible for checking when a hen was ready to lay, which meant inserting a finger inside the hen to feel if there was an egg on the way. This was known as 'trying the hen'. We all loved trying the hens, and would compete with one another for whose turn it was, because the lucky girl or boy to feel the egg would be the one who got to eat it. We only ate the hen herself when she got too old to lay or, the odd time, when we bought a hen at the market in the city. Hens were generally bought live and killed at home (the story you may have heard about a hen's body continuing to run for a period after the head has been cut off is actually completely true). For Christmas, Dad's family in Galway would send us down a fat goose or gander from the farm, but for meat – aside from game – we mostly ate locally raised and cured bacon.

Mam did all her cooking on an open fire, and she was very good at it, producing delicious home-made bread, stews, roast meats and more. Breads and cakes were made in a cast-iron pot, with embers piled up around it and on top of the lid. When salmon was in season, Mam would take a big hunk of the sweet, pink flesh, wrap it in a piece of silk, and poach it in creamy, unpasteurised milk, fresh from a local cow. It was so tasty, no sauce at all was really necessary, but Mam had her own gravy that she poured over it at the table.

As the salmon was worth a lot to sell, more often we ate the by-catch – the other, less valuable fish that had been caught in the net at the same time: bottom-feeding fish such as plaice, various other flatfish, and the odd time even herring – before my time, herring used to swim far up the river, until the electrical powerhouse changed the nature of the water, pushing the salt water further downstream. Many Coonagh families foraged for watercress in the local streams, but we did not particularly like it, so we stuck with cabbage.

As soon as I was big enough to scramble over a wall and run away from a cross dog, I contributed to the family diet by providing apples. From an early age, I took pride in the fact that there was no wall too high and no guard dog too fierce for me. Many's the day I came home, my face full of pride and my jumper lumpy with apples from a local farmer's trees. The odd time I would even spend a threepenny piece and get a bag of them honestly, although they never seemed to taste as good as the stolen ones.

Dad's work as a general labourer at the cement factory was physically demanding, but he always seemed to have enough energy left to fish during the season. Fishing for salmon in particular was a hugely important source of income for the families in Coonagh, especially those that were not land-owning. As soon as boys were big enough and strong enough, they would help their fathers in the industry, and we all learned from watching our parents how the business worked. Men and women alike also picked up casual work on local farms on the floodplains of the Shannon, where there was ample seasonal work weeding, gathering crops and digging dykes to drain the land and channel the water.

During the winter months, the golden reeds that lined the banks of the river were ready for harvesting. Locals used their traditional boats, known as gandelows, to gather them. Right of access to the reeds was determined according to an old law that associated given families with particular stretches of riverbank. This could, but did not always, correspond to owner-ship of the adjacent land. Dad was particularly good at gathering the reeds in the brick mud-ponds, which were man-made inlets left from when the brickworks had harvested mud from the banks, back in the nineteenth cen-tury. Like everyone else, he used the family gandelow to access them; the slight dip on the floor of the boat made it easy to slide along the mudflats while gathering reeds with a sickle. On land, we brought them home with our donkeys and carts, stripped them down and packed them into bundles, We used them to thatch our own homes, and also sold them to thatchers for the roofs of others.

As soon as we were old enough, we children were helping Mam and Dad in a wide variety of ways. I remember, from the age of five or six, going across the fields with Mam, a handful of her skirt held tightly in my little fist, to gather firewood along the banks of the Shannon. As we all used our fires to cook and to heat our homes and our water, keeping the fire going at all times was essential, and it was often a struggle, as few families had enough money to depend entirely on fuels such as coal. The driftwood that washed up on the riverbank was our primary source of firewood, and collecting it was practically a daily occupation. The women, and the children who helped them, were to be seen all morning long making the journey down to the riverbank and returning with a bag of wood over their shoulders, or even a long tree trunk carried between two or three.

Sometimes, when fuel was scarce or flooding made it impossible to gather driftwood, people went out in the dead of night and cut pieces of hawthorn or blackthorn from the hedgerows of local farms, just to have something to burn. This was a frequent source of contention between the people of the village and the landowners, who would – understandably – be very angry about holes in their hedges, through which livestock might escape.

I started school at about the age of six, at the national school in Meelick, several miles from Coonagh. At that time, many of the adults in Coonagh, particularly the older ones, were still unable to read and write, or could only do so at a very basic level. The children of Coonagh were lucky enough to have a school bus that took us there and back; I remember getting on it for the first time, and how five or six bigger kids had to drag me in and keep me there, because I felt that it would be much nicer to stay at home with Mammy. By the time I was going to school, there was a huge push nationwide to improve the general educational standards of Ireland. The State had hired hundreds of school inspectors, who made sure that the schools were doing what they were supposed to, and that laws about truancy were strictly enforced. Looking back now, I can see that this was a watershed era for education. Standards were quickly rising all over the country.

Ours was a smallish rural school, right beside Meelick Church, with facilities that could be described as modest at best: one big room, with older kids at one end and younger kids at the other, and one teacher for each group. The girls had an earth-closet toilet outside, but the boys got to water the line of trees at the perimeter of the playground when they needed to relieve themselves. I was good at school, but I can't say that attending it was an entirely pleasant experience, because in those days far too many teachers used violence and fear as means to control the children. One of the teachers terrified us all, and I can only imagine how difficult it must have been for the children who struggled with their lessons, and who were more frequently singled out to be slapped or beaten. Whenever a child was selected for a beating, the whole school day was disrupted, as all the other kids would sit and stare in horror at what was happening, worrying that they might be next. We all envied the altar boys who served in the church, as occasionally they would get taken away for a few days to attend to their sacred duties. They also got to skip classes, and were never beaten by the teachers – although of course, now one can't help but wonder what price they may have paid for that.

The best part of going to school was spending time with my closest friend, Gabriel Hickey, who was the same age as me. Gabriel was a wild, restless boy, who got up to mischief on the school bus in the morning, at school all day, and then again on the school bus on the way home. He could get away with anything, because he had a natural charm that he could turn on like a tap. Even the teachers often overlooked his many misdeeds, and they were notoriously quick to reach for the yardstick.

While I was good at maths and already had a technical bent from a very early age, I also enjoyed learning about the history and legends of Ireland, and we were given a very good grounding in all of that. I loved hearing about the grand adventures of legendary characters such as the hero Fionn mac Cumhaill, who was said to have gained his wisdom from the salmon of knowledge. The story of him roasting his salmon on a fire and touching the shiny skin when it bubbled in the heat resonated with all of us, as this was something that we had seen ourselves on many occasions. Most of our fathers were salmon fishermen, and we joked among ourselves that perhaps one of them might himself one day catch a salmon of knowledge – then we would have no trouble at all following our lessons. This story, along with growing up almost in the shadow of the fabled Ardnacrusha power station, seemed to connect us to something bigger than ourselves, to the very idea of the Irish nation.

As children growing up in a rural community, stories of the fantastic, the supernatural and the magical seemed much more plausible than they do today. Many of the adults we knew still took seriously the stories that were told about the mysterious funeral that had been seen entering the fairy fort located on the perimeter of our village (although others would dismiss these stories and say that the alleged witnesses had simply been drunk and were seeing things). Mam herself often warned me to stay away from a certain elder tree that was a well-known local landmark and for some reason associated with the fairies and with the idea of danger. She also often told me stories of the banshee, although I always had the impression that she did not give the banshee a lot of credence, especially because there were so many foxes in the area, whose cries sounded just like those of a wailing woman.

The salmon season started on the first of February and ended on the twenty-ninth of July, during which time the fishing boats spent twenty-four hours on the water, with men working shifts Monday to Friday; there was a State-imposed ban from six on Saturday morning to six on Monday morning, to give the fish a chance to get upriver to spawn. During the season, Dad took as much holiday time away from the cement factory as possible, and when he ran out of holidays, he simply did an additional shift of work on the boat once he had finished with the factory work. Before the season, fishing families got everything ready, and after the season they were already thinking about all they had to do to prepare for the next one.

There were always some people who fished outside the season and managed not to get caught, but Dad could see the sense in the legislation and in giving the fish a chance. He always obeyed the law and told his sons that they should do the same. Unlike a lot of the fishermen in the area, he looked on poaching with great disfavour too, and was careful only to fish in approved waters.

Salmon was the king of the fish, but for my money, the eel was nearly as good, and because there was less money to be made selling eels, we probably ate them more often. Atlantic eels, *Anguilla anguilla*, were caught with a hook or with a fine net, and they were delicious. My brother Tom used to keep a hook on the go to catch an eel whenever he was salmon fishing, and I remember him skinning one and using the skin to make a belt.

The eel is like a magical fish. On their birth in the Sargasso Sea in the Northern Atlantic Subtropical Gyre, they look like flower petals and not like any type of fish at all. They grow gradually, as the Gulf Stream carries them to Ireland. As they pass through a transparent phase and acquire the form of an eel, they are known as 'glass eels'. Only when they reach the rivers do they darken and start to swim and act in their own right, at which stage they are known as 'yellow eels'. As adults, they are large, slippery, highly intelligent and quite fearsome-looking creatures with a well-developed instinct for survival. They can live as yellow eels for more than twenty years, eating invertebrates and fish, before turning into silver eels and migrating back to the Sargasso Sea to repeat the cycle. Their reputation lives on in the phrase 'as slippery as an eel', meaning someone who is hard to pin down.

Fishing on the Shannon required a considerable investment of money and labour, and as most families in Coonagh had very modest incomes, a huge amount of planning went into getting everything lined up within budget. The traditional fishing boat of the area, the gandelow, was expensive, worth more than many hard-working men would make in a year. Even with careful maintenance, they had to be replaced quite frequently. Great thought went into selecting the boatbuilder; Dad swore by a family called Doran, who had been making boats in Limerick for generations.

Nets were made of hemp or cotton, which would deteriorate in quality. Although they could be repaired a certain number of times, they also had to be replaced frequently. This meant placing an order directly with the English firm Bridport-Gundry – by phone or post, or via an intermediary such as one of the fishmongers in the city or a door-to-door salesman representing the company. It was essential for the size of the mesh to be just right, because if it was too wide, fish could force their way through.

The various parts of the net – the net itself, and then the large buoys and the smaller cork floats – had to be assembled at home ahead of the season.

If you were very lucky, you might get two seasons, or a season and a half, out of a hemp net. Most families, if they could, purchased two brand new nets every season, in two different mesh sizes, and two sets of hemp rope to complete the kit. One net was for the larger spring salmon, the other for the smaller summer salmon. Each was worth more than most labouring men earned in a month.

Fishing licences also had to be purchased – they were easy to get, but they cost about three pounds, which was a significant sum for most people. For many, this outlay meant organising financing with the fishmonger whom they supplied with fish: he would advance the money, to be paid back over the course of the season – with interest. Relationships with fishmongers and with crew members were crucial and had to be maintained from one season to another.

Usually three men worked together, and as a majority of them also had other jobs, at one point or another most of the local men had worked with most others. During the frequent storms and squalls of the spring season, two men rowed the boat while the third paid out and pulled in the net, which was about a hundred and fifty yards long. During the summer season, when the weather was milder and storms much less frequent, you might manage with a crew of just two. In summer, boys from the age of twelve or thirteen were strong and resilient enough to do a full shift on the water, and sometimes even younger children were brought along. While most of those fishing for salmon were men and boys, a small number of women also joined crews and fished, usually the daughter or wife of one of the fishermen.

I remember my first trip out with Dad, when I was four or five. I was both nervous and excited, unsure of how to stand on the boat, which seemed to dip and slide beneath my feet, but proud to be included in the world of men and exhilarated at the sight of all the salmon that we landed. A few years later, aged eight or nine, I felt like a seasoned fisherman as, for the first time, I untangled a big, beautiful salmon from the net – they were captured when their gills became entangled – and killed it. 'Good man,' Dad said. '*Maith an fear thú*. Grand job.' Back at the house, I overheard him telling Mam what I had done. It was amazing.

Although fishing was part and parcel of ordinary life in Coonagh, it was also dangerous and sometimes tragic. I remember one rough, windy day, when I was seven or eight, the word went around that Willie Considine had been killed. It had really been too stormy to go fishing at all, and most of the men had stayed at home that day, but he and a friend had gone down anyway. A couple of hours after they went out, their boat was seen coming back in with just one man on board. Within minutes, everyone had heard the terrible news: Willie was dead.

Within an hour or two, we had all gathered in his family home to support the family. I remember it as if it were yesterday – standing beside my mother, part of a sombre crowd around the dead man, who lay stretched out on the floor of a home much like ours. His sou'wester hat was pulled over his face, covering the eyes that would never again scan the river and assess where to cast his nets. In that moment, I realised that, despite his abundance of caution, the same thing could easily happen to my own dad. Over the course of my life in Coonagh, the river has claimed the lives of fifty or sixty people. Once I came across one myself, with curiosity giving way to horror when I realised that what I had taken for the black pelt of a poor cat or dog was actually the back of a drowned man's head. On another occasion, I was happy to have given a local family closure when I found their missing loved one among the reeds six months after he disappeared.

Most of the fishermen took normal, sensible precautions to reduce the risk to themselves and anyone on board with them. All of them made efforts to be on the right side of God, with holy medals nailed inside the boat and little bottles of holy water regularly used to sprinkle the boat and crew. Water from the pilgrimage sites of Knock or even Lourdes was particularly prized. Mam swore by Knock water, and that is what Dad had on our boat. Getting the bottle of holy water ready at the start of the fishing season was considered just as important as getting in the nets and making repairs to the boat. In fact, for a lot of people, it was top of the list. Another precaution, this one intended to bring good luck to the fishing season, was bringing the nets into Limerick to be blessed by one of the priests at the Franciscan church. The fact that Jesus and His apostles had also been fishermen was not lost on the people of Coonagh. If it was good enough for Him, it was good enough for us.

Many of the river fishermen had also put in time at sea. They knew all the sailors' lore about good and bad luck, such as the idea that the man who owned a baby's caul would never drown. Dad would often let a salmon go if he had already caught enough for the day, or if it was on the small side: 'It'd be a sin to kill him,' Dad would say, meaning that we should give the small salmon a chance to grow up and make baby salmon of its own. But there were plenty who would never do that, believing that to release even one small salmon back into the wild might risk giving away their luck. I can't say that I paid those stories all that much attention, but they were always there in the background.

Certainly, as hard-working as they were, many of the fishermen also had a fatalistic streak that made them feel that fortune – good or bad alike – was largely determined by forces that they had only a limited ability to control. This fatalism may have contributed to the poor money management that was common among them. They often made quite big money during the salmon season, and then spent a lot of it in the pub, only to have to live very modestly for the rest of the year. It was often said that Coonagh should have been a much richer community than it was, but that much of our collective money ended up going down the drain, with the publicans of Limerick the primary beneficiaries of our hard work.

Most of what they made from their tireless labours went towards supporting the family, but there was enough left over for Mam and Dad to have a little fun with their friends. For Dad, this meant having a good bicycle, a Raleigh, that he could ride with his cycling club. Even years later, I would meet men in pubs who had stories to tell about Dad's exploits in cycling races: 'An awful aul' fecker!' they would say, good-humouredly. 'He tricked me out of a medal several times.' The races were all in good fun, and Dad was a very strong cyclist, who could go almost as quickly on his bike as people did in their cars along the winding counrty roads. Dad also loved greyhounds and used to race them, travelling as far as Galway at times to participate.

Mass on Sunday was an obligation for everybody, as were the periodic missions in the parish church in Meelick – priests actually came around the village to make sure that everyone was planning to attend. Both were, at least, also an opportunity to socialise and relax a little. The woman who had a new dress or hat would wear it, knowing all her friends and neighbours would be there to see her in her finery. We all went up to Mass on the bus, after which Dad would buy a few comics for us kids (the inspiration for our games of cowboys and Indians among the reed banks, and the start of my lifelong love of reading) while he and Mam chatted with their friends.

In those days, all of the comics came from England. They were stuffed with characters with stiff upper lips who killed their enemies without giving it a second thought. The enemies might be Germans, American Indians (as they were known in those days), or the Japanese or Koreans – the Korean War started in 1950, inspiring a wide range of children's literature describing the killing of 'kooks' and 'chinks'. Dad made it clear that he strongly disapproved of these comics and the messages they contained. I can see now that his buying them for us was a great measure of his love, because he knew how much we enjoyed them – he was prepared to put up with a certain amount of English propaganda in comic-strip form just to see the smiles on our faces as we turned the pages.

The missions, run by visiting preachers often from far-flung parts of the country such as Belfast, were a more serious affair than a regular Sunday Mass. My friends and I managed to enjoy them anyway, yelling out our responses to the prayers as loudly as we could: 'Do you renounce the devil and all his works?' 'YEH-WE-R'NOUNCE-DE-DIVIL-'N'-ALL-HIS-WORKS!' We would light all the candles available, earning a stern glance from the priest, who would be unsure whether or not we were mis-behaving, but would usually give us the benefit of the doubt. The local confraternity was dedicated to Blessed Oliver Plunkett, whose head is – we were told – on display in distant Drogheda. Participating in these missions could be a social outlet for some, as well as an occasion of piety.

My initial enthusiasm for these extracurricular religious activities waned with the years. I was always upset about the little 'killeen' – the unconse-crated graveyard where the bodies of unbaptised children were laid to rest – located opposite a friend's house, where several of his own siblings were buried. Inside the site's boundaries there was a yellow-washed thatched house, home to Mick Bunce and his wife, Ellen. They had lost their only child, Joseph, when he was just twenty-one. Joseph had been swimming in the Shannon after a hard day's work one day in the mid-1920s when suddenly he had gone under, and nobody had been able to save him. One of the men who tried was Jack 'Scotch' Hickey, a good friend of Dad's. Now very elderly, the Bunces lived all alone with only the souls of the stillborn infants buried all around them for company. We were told that the babies had to be buried apart from Christian people because their souls had not been cleansed by baptism, so they would never be able to enter Heaven. That never seemed fair to me, when they were so small, and life so fragile. It was very sad for my friend's mam, who saw her own children's burial places every time she left her house.

Local lore also maintained that two English soldiers – who had possibly been involved with the drawing of the first set of Ordnance Survey maps in the early 1800s, when the Shannon area had been very carefully sur-veyed – had been murdered by local men and buried secretly in the killeen alongside the infants, their heathen English graves marked by a large stone or stones. Our history as a people was not just spoken of frequently; it was written into the landscape we inhabited.

When I look back at the amount of freedom my friends and I enjoyed as children, I feel utterly astonished by it. We were all taught about the dangers of our local area, in particular the dangers associated with the Shannon itself, which regularly claimed the lives of fishermen and of others who were careless or unlucky. But then we were let loose to play and trusted to keep ourselves alive. Long before Mam considered me big enough to play out on my own, I followed the bigger lads around, joining in their games even when they did not want me to. Sometimes we would make our way to Cratloe, a village several miles away along the railway, with a GAA pitch (there was no team in Coonagh; ours was banned because our local pride had spilled over into violence one time too many).

Mainly though, the banks and floodplains of the Shannon were our playground. In the river mud we found countless treasures – buoys that had gone adrift; broken bits of china; a cellulose doll's head, its round blue eyes hinting at what it must have seen. In the fields and in the old brick factory, where Coonagh mud had for generations been baked into the clay bricks that built Limerick, we played endless games and we built little dens and houses for ourselves. Perhaps because we had all half-overheard adults' conversations about the relatively recent past – 1916, the Irish War of Independence and all the rest of it – occasionally we interrupted our cowboys and Indians games for spirited debates about whether the Indians really were the baddies or whether they had been like some of our grandparents and the lads we had read about in school who had justly taken up arms against an oppressor. We never really reached a conclusion, and were extremely vague on the details of how the West was won, but as a result of these exchanges, sometimes we would switch things around and play the game differently, with the Indians as the goodies and the cowboys carrying on in a treacherous manner. We would enact lingering, noisy, cowardly, Englishy deaths.

On a day when I did not have school, I spent most of my time playing on the riverbank. As the sun set and the sky grew dark, I would find secret hiding places, because I knew it was time to go to bed, and I never wanted to do that. Among the reeds I would crouch, the smell of the Shannon filling my nostrils, while around me I could hear the nocturnal animals – otters, riverside rats – beginning to stir and go about their business and the waterbirds settling in for the night.

Some years before, many of the local children had gone barefoot out of necessity, because their parents could not afford shoes. I always had a pair of perfectly good shoes on the go, but in the summer, I preferred to kick them off, because I liked the way the earth felt, warm and springy beneath my feet. I especially enjoyed the dampness of it against my bare skin on those evenings on the riverbank. Eventually, reluctantly, when I started getting cold, I would make my way home and crawl into bed alongside my brothers, the Shannon mist still drying on my skin. The next morning, as soon as I had eaten breakfast, I would be back.

I remember as if it were yesterday standing on the banks of the Shannon as a child, watching the sunlight glint on the waves and looking forward to the day when I would be big enough to have a gandelow of my own. I would join the men, whose standing in the local community was determined largely by their prowess on the water and the number of salmon they managed to land.

'Keep your focus at school,' Dad often advised me. 'You're a clever young fella. You pay attention to your lessons and you'll be able to get a good job, something better than catching fish.'

I did pay attention to my lessons and, despite the violence of some of the teachers, I was good at school and quite liked it – but I paid no attention to my dad's advice about fishing. By the time I was old enough to dream of joining the men and my older brothers, the Shannon was my favourite place to be, and hunting salmon was my dream.

I had no idea then that our way of life was threatened, and had been for years. No idea that, upstream, the Ardnacrusha station was chopping countless eels into tiny little pieces as they passed through its turbines, that pitifully few salmon were managing to get past it and upstream to their spawning grounds, and that the few salmon young that did manage to hatch also had to pass through the turbines on their way to the sea, which killed most of them.

The ESB had constructed a salmon-trapping weir, the Thomond Weir, which straddled the entire River Shannon as it passed through Limerick City. The weir was constructed at a cost of £35,000 – an immense sum. It was declared complete in 1940, and hailed as one of the most modern weirs in Europe.[83] It was used to monitor salmon from 1940 and was in 'full working order' by the summer of 1942,[84] the year before I was born. The ESB also used the weir for commercial salmon fishing, selecting about 25 per cent of the prime salmon in the river and selling them on to markets in England and further afield.

The fishing community knew that things were different from before, but were unaware of just how bad they were going to get. In 1944, when I was a toddler, just starting to walk, researchers reported that the run of salmon on the river was about 30 per cent less than normal, and that the average weight of the fish taken at the Thomond Weir was down by a very significant two pounds.[85] Further studies showed a very significant decrease in the number of salmon in the river, with fish also now tending to run in the summer rather than the spring. The Shannon Scheme provided the only explanation for the dramatic changes in numbers and behaviour.[86]

The fish that did manage to reach their spawning beds now also found that conditions had changed, or were so exhausted after the effort required to cross a weir or fish pass that they were confused and disorientated, more than usually vulnerable to predators and to stress-related disease, and less likely to reach their destinations.[87] But the State and the ESB were one and the same; there was an urgent need for Ireland to modernise, and the loss of fish and other species along the way, and the degradation of habitats, was seen as a price worth paying.

Back then, as a child growing up in a fishing community, I had no awareness of the technological and material advances that were already beginning to transform the fishing industry from a traditional practice in balance and harmony with the natural environment to one in which human predators could take ever more, beyond all need or reason. A fish population that was already more threatened than anyone realised was decimated, and my community was utterly transformed in too many ways to count.

CHAPTER THREE

Taking to the Water

By the time I was nine or ten, I was getting big enough to dream of being a crew member on board a fishing gandelow, not just a snotty kid trying to go along for the ride. I lived for the days when Dad was not busy at the cement factory and would let me get involved in the fishing. I had caught my first fish out with Dad when I was just eight or nine, but I was still judged too small to participate on a regular basis in the more serious fishing. Generally, Dad and a crew of men, or Dad and my older brothers, would go out, leaving me at home with Mam and the little ones.

Once I was judged to have a modicum of sense, I was allowed to go down to the riverbank to help when they went out, and then again when they came in. This was better than nothing, but I longed for the day when I would be pushing out in the boat as a fully fledged crew member, waving goodbye to the poor aul' eejits left gawping at us from the riverbank, and heading off for an adventure on the water.

In the meantime, my good pal Gabriel and I made the best of it. Our favourite spot was an area called Jack Liston's Bridge, where a small bridge spanned a little tributary, the Crompaun River, feeding the Shannon. We loved playing there. In those days, the shallow water of the tributary was filled with smolts, sea trout and croneen, a type of freshwater trout whose name comes from the Irish *crón,* which means dark yellow or tawny and refers to their distinctive colour.

The Crompaun was a short little river – the name comes from the Irish *crompán,* meaning a small river or stream – that ran from up near my national school in Meelick to where it entered the Shannon, near Coonagh, right along the border between County Limerick and County Clare. On a fine day, it was tantalising to sit in the classroom, knowing that it was just outside.

Now that we were getting older and bolder, once in a while Gabriel, his brother Junior, our pal Noel and I gave ourselves a day off school and spent it playing in the Crompaun. When one day we found a flattish canoe, apparently abandoned, near the Crompaun, a plan quickly formed. The next day, instead of getting on the bus to school, we stashed our books under a hedge, retrieved the boat and dragged it up to the mouth of the Crompaun. We devised a grand plan to float our boat all the way to Meelick, where we could mount a daring raid. We would rescue some of our friends from the classroom and take them off for a spin on our boat. We were delighted with ourselves, thinking about how impressed all our friends would be when they looked out the windows of the school and saw us boyos floating by.

The water in the Crompaun was very shallow and the tide was out, and even though our canoe was flat-bottomed and shallow, it was very difficult to get it to move upstream. Finally, we settled on the laborious technique of building dams out of mud and stone. These allowed the water to build up enough that we could push our boat forward eight or ten yards at a time. Wading in muddy water up to our thighs, we spent the entire day doing this.

Eventually we had to relinquish our dream of reaching Meelick – even after many hours of work, we had only managed to move the canoe a hundred yards or so. It did not really matter. It had been an absolutely wonderful day. We waded out of the Crompaun and stood on the bank, looking at each other. We were all soaking wet, covered in mud and rosy-cheeked from the physical work. We used our filthy hands to straighten our jumpers and push back our sweaty hair, and told one another that if we spun a convincing yarn about what the teacher had said in school that day, our mammies wouldn't notice a thing. We headed off to retrieve our books and go home.

When we got home that evening, we all told our mothers that we had been in school. None of them believed us. 'You were in your eye in school,' Mam said. 'Look at you – you're ruined. You're destroyed.' Mam made me change my clothes and held me down firmly with one hand while she gave me a good scrubbing with the other. The other lads were subjected to the same indignities by their own mothers. The next morning at school, the teacher had somehow got to hear about our escapade, and we all got a good walloping with his yardstick to teach us a lesson. He had been trained with the Christian Brothers, and there was nothing he did not know about corporal punishment and how to administer it. The walloping was not fun and our parents were unsympathetic when we complained later that day: 'That'll learn you, you'll think again the next time.' But we kids agreed that, despite everything, our day out had been worth it.

While actually going fishing with the big lads and the grown men was the dream, doing whatever I could for the fishermen was the second-best thing. Because they would be out for hours, the crew had to bring a packed meal with them. I helped to carry it down – sandwiches of salmon or ham, carefully wrapped in newspaper that transferred its black print onto the soft white bread so clearly you could read the headlines with each bite; a bottle of tea with milk and sugar, stuffed into an old sock to keep it warm, or at least warmish, until they were ready to drink it. Flasks, which kept the tea properly warm, started coming in from the mid-1950s and were very popular among the fishermen, who appreciated a warm drink in a cold boat. Some of the fishermen would sneak in a bottle of stout or two, perhaps when their wives were not looking.

'A bottle of stout,' Dad said, 'can be a great comfort to a man during a long wait on the river, with a cold wind whipping about his face.'

The men wore layers and layers of clothes to stay warm during the long hours of fishing: woollen undercoats, thick flannel shirts, jumpers and heavy overcoats that became sodden in the rain. Over their trousers they wore leggings oiled with pig fat to keep their legs as dry as possible, and on their heads they wore sou'wester hats. On their feet they wore heavy leather boots, often with hobnails, with waterproof gaiters over them. Under the boots, their feet were encased in woollen socks – the heavier the better, but not always in the best of condition; I remember seeing lots of pink toes through holes in the men's socks when the boots came off.

The waterproof gear was generally made of thick calico and oiled at home. Modern gear that was more waterproof was starting to become available, but it was expensive, so to save money a lot of people stuck with the clothing they had always known. Reluctant as they were to spend money on themselves and their comfort, no expense was spared when it came to the equipment used for catching salmon. The hemp nets, which lasted for a year or two, were purchased from the best provider, and eye-watering sums were expended when a gandelow had to be purchased from a boatbuilder.

It was thrilling to watch the boat come to shore after hours out on the river. It was easy to see when the men had had a good expedition, because the gandelow, which was slung low in the water anyway because of how it was constructed, would be sitting even lower with the weight of the fish. Sometimes there were open-topped hessian bags of fish spread out over the nets. Gabriel and I would be leppin' up and down on the bank watching the men come in, as though we had not seen them for months. Each time was as exciting as the last. If they had had a good catch, everyone was in a great mood. 'Ah, we only got one!' someone would call out, laughing. 'A rotten aul' day!' That was their way of saying that they had actually caught loads, because when they really had a bad day, they were sullen and tired and did not want to talk about it. Next thing they would be pulling into the land, jumping out and piling their haul onto the grass, where it lay shining silver in the sunlight.

Gabriel and I were always mad to carry as much as we could manage on our backs, to take part in the triumphant parade of successful fishermen from the Shannon through the fields to their homes. With a heavy fish or two weighing me down, I was almost as proud as if I had caught the salmon myself. I hoped that by showing Dad that I was big and strong and capable of working hard, I would be allowed out with the men.

Eventually, when I was about ten, and quite big and sturdy for my age, I heard those sacred words: 'Ah, sure, maybe he could come out with us on the water the next time,' and saw some approving nods issued in my direction. My heart nearly burst out of my chest as I tried to play it cool and not let on how excited I was. This was the biggest thrill of my young life – better than the birth of a new baby in the family; better than my First Holy Communion with its new suit, its few bob from the neighbours and the fond smiles of Mam and Dad; better even than the last day of school before we were let out for the summer. Getting big enough to go out on the water with Dad and the others was all my dreams come true.

Now I could go with Dad and my brothers, or with one of the neighbours if someone was putting together a crew and was a little short. Picking up the gear and heading down to the water with the rest of them was a brilliant feeling. I was one of the men now, and the others saw me as someone who knew about and understood the salmon just as they did.

Of course, I was regularly reminded of the dangers inherent in fishing. There were many stories of tragic accidents, and my parents were very good at relating them. Even stories about those who had died years before were frequently aired, no detail too small or too awful to be recounted. Back in the 1920s, for example, a local fisherman, Jack, went missing, Despite the community searching for days, he was nowhere to be found. About a week later, his brother and his crew went out fishing at about ten at night, catching the tide. When they raised their net the first time, it was much heavier than expected. Hauling it together, they pulled it on board and realised that they had taken in poor Jack's body. He had been submerged for a week and no longer looked like himself, but there was no mistaking him.

The men lowered their dead companion reverently into the front of the boat and pulled a tarpaulin over him; there was no way for them to get home until the water rose again. For eight hours, they fished out the tide, piling up the glittering fish over Jack's prone corpse. The fish flipped and wriggled on Jack's still body until they drowned in the air and became still too. When the sun rose in the morning, the group brought the fish and the dead man home. There was no disrespect in what they had done. On the contrary, everyone in the community knew that it was what Jack would have wanted. They were glad that he got to fish one last time before he was laid to rest. It was a little comfort for the family at such a painful time.

Soon Gabriel and I, every chance we got, were borrowing boats from the men and going out fishing on our own. Never mind that we were still only half-grown boys; we both had a knack for fishing and earned the respect of our elders. The Shannon and its riverbanks had always been our playground, and now we were so comfortable in and on it that it was also our home. On a sunny day in April, we jumped in for a swim a good two months before anyone else was brave enough, telling each other that we were setting a record. We were both strong swimmers, like a pair of young otters, but Gabriel was even better than me. He confidently swam further from the bank and would dive boldly under the water, coming up with his dark hair slick against his head and the drops of water on his bare shoulders sparkling in the spring sunlight.

I soon became expert at understanding and observing the spoken and unspoken rules of the fishing community. The salmon fisheries of the Shannon had been subject to formal legislation, local and national, for hundreds of years, and it was important to keep abreast of what the rules were, as getting done for poaching or otherwise breaking the law could be an expensive business. About sixty miles of the river overall was open to net-fishing. Our territory was quite big – all the way from Coonagh to the Fergus estuary, about twenty miles away across the river from Foynes Island and the town of Foynes. Nobody owned the river, so we had to share it. This meant that boats stayed a particular distance from one another, respecting the other crew's space and rights over a certain area of water at a particular point in the tide.

There were formal rules and regulations, but most importantly, there was a certain code of conduct. The Shannon Estuary fished by the people of Coonagh was divided into 'drifts'. These reached from Coonagh Point to the mouth of the River Fergus, which is one of the main tributaries of the Shannon, entering its estuary at Ennis, County Clare. The various drifts recognised by Coonagh fishermen were referred to by names that you will not find on any map, such as 'the Dead Woman's Hand' and 'Ballymorris and the Mud', each with its respective backstory. Over countless generations, the etiquette and social rules associated with the fishing had gradually developed.

Because of the constantly changing nature of the river environment, the rules could be quite complicated. For example, you might cast out your drift net at a certain point, but its location would change depending on factors beyond your control, including the movements of the tide, the nature of the currents and the wind. This meant that ensuring your net stayed sufficiently distant from other people's was a constant effort. A careful watch had to be kept over it, and it had to be moved when necessary. This situation would be multiplied countless times over as all the different gandelows, with their respective fishing crews, took to the water and slotted into place.

People generally observed all of the complex etiquette around salmon fishing. When they did not, they heard about it soon enough from the others. Those who broke the largely unspoken rules attracted huge disapproval and anger from the rest of the community.

Impatience was the source of most bad behaviour on the water. A fishing crew might have set themselves up for the day and then waited for hours without catching a single fish. Eventually they would say, 'Feck this,' and move to another spot, in the hope that it would be more favourable. As this often involved infringing on someone else's fishing grounds for the day, tempers could flare. It was understandably frustrating for the second crew, who had probably also been fishing for hours, when someone swept in and placed their own net to the fore, catching all the fish that should rightfully have belonged to the more patient outfit of fishermen.

Things could potentially become dangerous, as two or more gandelows could jostle for position in the middle of the fast-moving river, with oars being wielded to exchange blows and harsh words raining in from all sides. It is not easy to stand upright in a gandelow and swing an oar with sufficient force to knock a competitor overboard, or to break his paddle in two, but I have seen both things happen with my own eyes. Some men intentionally broke their own oar in half to make a shorter, more wieldable weapon, with a view to actually inflicting serious harm on a competitor. That was downright nasty, and could result in a man spending several weeks in hospital recovering from his injuries.

Very violent encounters like these did not happen often, so when they did, they were talked about for years, the gruesome details embellished in each retelling. They rarely resulted in a court trial, and the few that did rarely resulted in a conviction, because it was all but impossible for a judge to know whom to believe, and because everyone knew each other so well they would be reluctant to testify against one another. At the end of the day, no matter what had happened on the water, they were all friends and neighbours – sometimes relatives too – and expected to spend the rest of their days living in close proximity to one another.

Nonetheless, there were times – generally after a few pints had been taken – when someone's former transgression, perhaps even from years before, would spark harsh words. There were even times when those harsh words could lead to a fight. As a result, plenty of the salmon fishermen of Coonagh were barred from pubs all over Limerick, although most of them were quite good at sneaking in, and they were all good customers after being paid by the fishmonger. (I am glad to report that I have personally refrained from ever getting physical, although I have occasionally surprised even myself with the strong language coming from my mouth.)

Being on the boat with Dad was always special for me. Not just because of the excitement of catching the fish and the thrill of being considered big enough to do it, but also because these were the times when I felt closest to him. Dad worked so hard that when he came home in the evenings he was tired and needed to rest. But when we were on the water and the nets were out, we had prolonged periods of time to sit and talk. This was when Dad told me all his stories about growing up in Galway and the things his family had got up to. It was when I felt closest to him. The long hours on the water made it possible for me to get to know Dad on a whole new level. On the water, waiting for the fish, a contemplative mood would take him and he would relate stories about his childhood, his IRA activities before and after my birth, and much more. I treasured those times with Dad and the fact that, as I got older, he felt increasingly open to speak with me about everything that was going on in his life and everything that preoccupied him.

Dad was still fiercely republican when I was growing up in the 1950s. He would read any newspaper, but was particularly fond of *The Irish Press*, which related the news from the viewpoint of Éamon de Valera and his party. Even though the IRA was illegal now, Dad saw no difference between the IRA before 1922 and the IRA after it, and continued to support its political aims all his life. In 1957, when I was thirteen, Limerick man Seán South was shot and killed during an IRA raid on an Ulster Constabulary barracks in Brookborough, County Fermanagh. Seán had been very active in Limerick republican circles generally, and thousands of people, including the then Mayor of Limerick City, Ted Russell, attended his funeral. Dad had known Seán very well, and he and I were there too. Dad was one of the ushers, telling the mourners where they should sit in the church. Seán's funeral meant a lot to Dad, and so it meant a lot to me too. It remains an important memory.

* * *

The fishermen of Coonagh were increasingly concerned about the ongoing drop in the salmon population, and the scientific community and government gradually became worried too. While a decline in the number of fish had been anticipated from the start, the situation was far worse than anyone expected, and the government eventually realised that it had to act.

Parteen Weir, constructed back in the 1920s, was still a very impressive structure thirty years later. Made of reinforced concrete, it had four double roller gates, each ten metres wide, and two single roller gates, each measuring eighteen metres. The original fish pass, with its thirteen steps, had been failing to save the salmon from decimation from as soon as it opened.

Meanwhile, three decades after construction on the Ardnacrusha power station was completed, Ireland was starting to see dividends from its investment in electricity. While it remained a predominately agricultural nation, now that they could count on a reliable source of electricity, industries were steadily starting to grow, even in areas far away from traditional centres of commerce. More and more towns and villages had electricity, and the rural electrification scheme was starting to light up the countryside. It powered agricultural and domestic machinery, making life easier for people like farmers and housewives, who had previously had to spend all their days engaged in tough, physical work. Although parents still had to pay school fees if they wanted their children to continue their studies past primary school, more people were now completing secondary, and even going to university – often with financial assistance in the form of a county council grant. There was a growing number of trained professionals working in jobs like engineering, agricultural science and academia.

Locally, Shannon Airport was probably the most prominent symbol of the changes happening across Ireland and the new opportunities that were opening up. The airport – which, like all major businesses in the area, would not have existed without Ardnacrusha power station up the road – had opened in 1939, and from 1945 it was active as Ireland's first transatlantic airport. On the fringes of western Europe, Ireland was ideally located for planes to stop off and refuel on their way to America.

By the 1950s, the airport, and a variety of industries supplying it with goods and services, employed large numbers of locals. Many of these, in previous generations, would probably have followed their fathers into the Shannon fisheries, or would simply have emigrated. While emigration levels remained high in the 1950s, the airport was a sign that perhaps change was coming. To a lot of people then, I suppose the ongoing damage to the environment, and particularly to the fish populations of the Shannon, would have seemed a price worth paying for progress, if they thought about it at all. The 1950s was still a tough time, but advances in technology were setting the scene for rapid development down the line. The idea of a world in which most Irish people were not struggling was starting to take shape. By the 1950s, Irish demand for electricity was forty times greater than it had been in 1930, less than a generation before.[88]

In 1956, Mam and Dad were given the option of moving out of the one-room house where they had spent all their married life so far and renting a new council house with modern conveniences. They would have running water, indoor sanitation and – finally! – electricity, provided to us, as to so many others, by the vast turbines at Ardnacrusha. At the time, families could obtain a site from a local farmer, and then approach the council with a view to having a house built. Mam used to milk for one of the local farming families, the Hickeys, and when she approached them to ask about a site, they were extremely helpful. About six homes, designed by Limerick architect Patrick J Sheahan, were built in Coonagh under this new scheme.

In most respects, the new house was modelled on a fairly traditional one-storey Irish farmhouse, but Patrick Sheahan incorporated an unusual round porthole-style window in the lobby, just to the right of the door when you looked at it from the front. I do not know why, but I would like to think that he had in mind the long tradition of Coonagh men going to sea. In any case, it was a nice touch, a little whimsy in an otherwise practical home. Mam and Dad had worked very hard to bring home a salary and to provide us all with a happy childhood and all the comforts possible, and it had always been very tough. The new house, with a kitchen, a living room, a bathroom and several bedrooms, as well as a fine slate roof, represented a huge improvement in the whole family's quality of life, but especially Mam's.

The new house was just down the road from the old one, and I can still remember how we carried our furniture and other belongings down, piece by piece. That was an exciting day. Somehow in the changeover, or perhaps a while before, baby Margaret's grave-marker, which had both fascinated and upset me as a little boy, got left behind. I know that Mam and Dad never forgot her, but perhaps this was indicative of the family feeling positive, looking towards the future rather than the past. Certainly, Mam in particular was always keen to adopt modern technologies and ways of doing things. As someone who had done extremely physically hard work all her life, she was not one to be overly sentimental about the old ways of doing things. She was in favour of change when she could see that it was for the better.

From the new house, Dad and the boys – including me – continued to fish. At times, Dad came home with hundreds of glittering salmon, which he tipped out on the floor to sort before the merchant came to buy them for sale in Limerick City. The numbers were down a lot compared to a few decades before, but there still seemed to be enough to go around. By now, aged fourteen, I am sure that I already knew more about salmon than most marine biologists at the university.

Mam and Dad, like almost everyone of their generation, had only been to primary school. I progressed to secondary at the Tech in Limerick City, which was an excellent school. I did not completely realise it at the time, but I was part of a huge cultural shift in Ireland, a member of the first generation to have plenty of options. Although I suppose in some ways we were kept down by quite a repressive State and religious culture, in another way we were being given a glimpse of tremendous freedoms.

Even the prospect of emigrating – still on the cards for countless young Irish people – felt different than before. Those who went off to England or America were increasingly doing so with educational standards as high or higher than those they found there. Irish people abroad were no longer at the bottom of the social heap and emigration could be viewed in a positive light, as an opportunity for adventure and for getting on in life. I feel very lucky to have had the best of both worlds: a training since childhood in the traditional ways of the Shannon fishery, but also the opportunity to get a decent education, to learn in the sort of educational setting that most Irish people of my parents' generation had never been able to avail of.

At school, I enjoyed the practical subjects like woodwork and metalwork, and the logic-based ones like maths and mechanical drawing. I loved Irish too, partly because I had learned a decent amount of it from Dad, who was a native speaker. As a lad from Coonagh, I came in for a certain amount of teasing from the Limerick City boys, who considered themselves much more sophisticated than yokels like me. At the weekends, when I was out cycling with Dad – it was illegal to fish on Saturdays and Sundays – my townie classmates would be parading around town in their Teddy-boy gear of drainpipe trousers, natty waistcoats, velvet-trimmed jackets and greased-back hair. They listened to rock and roll and eyed the girls, with Woodbine cigarettes dangling from the corners of their mouths, thinking that they looked like James Dean, whom all the girls fancied.

After a while, when they realised they could not get a rise out of me and that I could hold my own, some of the self-same Teddy boys were lining up to come out in the gandelow with me during the summer months, because they envied the freedom and the sense of adventure that I had taken for granted all my life. Truth be told, I felt sorry for them, growing up on the hard streets of Limerick, playing around lamp posts and street railings rather than on the river and among the fields and reed beds on either side of it.

My teachers were supportive of me in my studies, and I sometimes thought of pursuing a technical career. Mam and Dad wanted me to pre-pare for a trade or a profession, to get a qualification so that I would have an easier life than them. But I was also spending more and more time on the water. From childhood, I had been fishing full-time during the school holidays, working on the water until the river was as familiar as my own home, and supplementing the family income with what I caught. The thought of a career as an engineer or mechanic was enticing, but the call of the Shannon was stronger, and the river was where I really wanted to be. I thought of the men I had known all my life, whose knowledge of the Shannon and all she contained was so profound that they could tell at a glance which tributary a salmon came from, and I knew that what I wanted most was to learn from them.

We had always had a good social life with neighbours and relatives in the old house, but the new house was bigger and more comfortable and more easily facilitated large gatherings for activities like card-playing. I got very good at playing bridge, which was introduced to the community by the men who periodically left to do stints as deep-sea sailors. They learned how to play every card game imaginable during the long nights at sea. Some of the older men had been in the First World War, and had endless stories to tell about their experiences and about comrades of theirs who had paid the ultimate price and never came home.

I was getting into sports, too. In those days, older people with republican views still looked askance on games like soccer and rugby, which they saw as 'foreign' games. Youngsters like me were often happy to play both GAA and those games too, and really did not see any problem or conflict between enjoying them all. The old GAA ban on following English games was increasingly irrelevant to us anyway, as we could listen to any game we wanted to on the wireless. Before an important match that we really wanted to hear, we made sure to take the wireless's battery to the garage, to get its acid level fully topped up.

* * *

The idea of a salmon hatchery at Ardnacrusha, in which young salmon could be artificially raised, had been first mooted well before the construction of the power station. It would not be the first salmon hatchery in Ireland, but it would be by far the most ambitious. Some small-scale hatcheries had operated as early as 1864, but all they did was hatch the eggs and release them into the wild as soon as they had developed into fry.[89]

Even then, some people were aware of the health risks that this would pose to the salmon. A local fishmonger, Denis Hayes, was quoted in the *Limerick Leader* as saying that, at the time, Shannon salmon and trout were free of disease, but that this could change quickly if diseased ova were introduced to the river from outside sources.[90]

In 1923, the Department of Fisheries had stated that it would welcome the creation of a hatchery on the Shannon to improve the stock of salmon in the river.[91] In 1931, the idea of creating a hatchery linked to the power station was put forward on the grounds that the Shannon Scheme was likely to render the spawning grounds of the salmon 'useless', with a hatchery the only way in which 'the loss could be made good'.[92] Starting in 1952, works were carried out at the Parteen Weir to develop a salmon hatchery, which was operational from 1959. A fish pass lift was built – a circular, concrete structure at the generating end of the head race dam. The fish would enter at the bottom, and the lift would rise to the top as it filled with water. This was supposed to make it easier for the salmon to cross the weir and reach their spawning grounds.

The first run through the Ardnacrusha fish pass took place in 1959. The hope was that the salmon, hatched at Parteen Weir from eggs that were often imported from overseas or introduced from other Irish rivers, would stabilise the population in the river and bring a halt to a situation that was increasingly turning into an environmental emergency.

The local fishing community was delighted that the government was taking their concerns seriously at last. They were very hopeful that the Parteen Weir hatchery would repopulate the river and that the fish lift pass would make it sustainable again. On paper, it all looked positively wonderful. The country's top fishery experts explained that the fish could be hatched at Parteen Weir, kept there until they were smolts, and then lifted and dropped at various points along the river. They would then engage in the salmon's normal life cycle and journey, keeping the Shannon and Atlantic waters stocked with healthy salmon, and the areas around them full of thriving fishing communities. It would be the best of science and tradition coming together.

The hatchery at Parteen was the biggest of its kind in Ireland and Britain, producing 200,000 smolts every year.[93] To keep track of how many fish caught in the Shannon came from the hatchery, ESB workers removed the fish's adipose fins. These are small, fleshy fins that grow on the top and towards the back of a small number of fish species, including salmon, trout and catfish. Although the adipose fin may serve to help fish manoeuvre more effectively in rough waters, they can still manage very well without it, and removing it was an easy way for hatcheries to identify their fish without harming them. At least at first, the new hatchery and fish pass did seem to be helping. Quite quickly, the average salmon run had risen to 45,000, compared to 20,000 a decade before.

Many of the Shannon fishermen were extremely enthusiastic about the hatchery, and optimistic that not only would their own catches rebound, but that their children would be able to remain in the area, working in the same fishing grounds that had supported their families for generations. Dad did not share their positivity, and continued to advise me and the rest of the family to seek employment in another sector. No matter what grand things the ESB said about the hatchery and how it was going to restock the Shannon waters, he had his doubts.

It turned out that Dad was right. At first, it seemed as though the hatchery was working, as huge numbers of smolts were released into the river. Within just a few years, the artificially raised hatchlings – known as ranched fish – outnumbered the wild salmon considerably. The problem was that they did not behave like them. When they were released, they died in larger numbers than wild fish. They often failed to reproduce, while also competing for resources with the diminishing population of wild salmon. This made the stock of salmon progressively more dependent on the artificially bred fish, making a dire situation steadily worse.

I remember, at that time, helping Dad to remove tags from the dorsal fins of some of the fish he caught, which he was then able to exchange for a financial reward – he must have been taking part in some of the surveys of the fish population that were ongoing at that time. (The first systematic tagging of salmon started in Scotland in 1825, and was quickly established as a means by which the otherwise mysterious peregrinations of the salmon could be understood; tagging remains an important research tool to this day.) When Dad emptied out a load of fish on the floor, I helped to look for the tags and was hugely excited whenever I found one, because I was entitled to a share of the reward, which was a princely five shillings.

The new house, and the changes in lifestyle that it brought, and the hatchery with its grand promise of repopulating the Shannon with salmon, were two signs among many of the rapid modernisation taking place all over Ireland at that time, as I slipped from boyhood into manhood. Nearby Shannon Airport was busy, taking Irish emigrants to new lands and new opportunities and providing local employment. It also brought in tourists from all over the world, many of them anxious to experience the beautiful landscapes of the west of Ireland, and to go on fishing trips on Ireland's clean waters.

From the age of sixteen or so, I had a part-time job as a pump attendant at a petrol station on the Ennis Road. There, I met thousands of tourists – Americans, English and visitors from continental Europe – who had arrived in Ireland via Shannon Airport. Many of them were anglers, armed with impressive arrays of state-of-the-art fishing rods. They were here to fish for the beautiful, big Irish salmon they had heard so much about. They all seemed very excited and happy to be in Ireland. They would remark that they loved my accent, and many of them gave me generous tips when I filled up their tanks and gave their windscreens a bit of a wipe with the rag I kept in my back pocket. It made me realise how we in Ireland took the beauties of nature all around us very much for granted.

Unlike us net fishermen, the anglers used hooks. They may have brought their own from wherever they came from, but they also made a point of buying some in Limerick. Limerick was said to produce the best hooks for salmon angling in the entire world – hooks so sturdy and well-crafted that they would never bend or straighten under the weight of a large salmon, as inferior English products ('made of cast-steel, in imitation of Irish ones … the worst of all'[94]) were known to do. The original fishing hooks of Limerick were known as O'Shaughnessy fish hooks, and in the early nineteenth century, they had been renowned in Ireland and far afield: 'the best hooks in the world … at a trifling expense'.[95] It was said that no hook-maker outside Limerick was capable of imitating them, although many tried.

The hooks were made of cast steel. During the first stage of manufacture, they were handled by nail-makers, who heated them to a specific temperature, and no more, in a turf fire. They were then beaten out and brought to the hook-maker, who transformed them into hooks and tempered them. By the time I came along, hooks were generally imported, although the good reputation of the Limerick hook continued to linger. (The building where the hooks were once made can still be seen in Limerick city, beside the Franciscan church – at the time of writing, it sells flowers as 'O'Shaughnessy's Florist'.)

The tourists with all their expensive fishing hooks did not know what I had an inkling of – that in our rivers and streams, the situation for the salmon and many other species was not nearly as good as it should have been. Still, the Inland Fisheries Trust and Bord Fáilte, the Irish tourism authority, promoted fishing holidays in Ireland, and listed the Shannon and its tributaries as one of the main attractions. Did the visiting fishermen know, or care, that more and more of the fish available were no longer truly wild, but instead were ranched fish from the ESB hatcheries? Perhaps they did not even understand the difference. A lot of people did not.

Dad had been right to doubt the stories of how the salmon hatchery at Parteen Weir was going to save the day. It was increasingly clear to the fishing communities, who knew the waters better than anyone, that the government's efforts to repopulate the Shannon were failing. The authorities released millions of artificially raised smolts into the water every year, and almost all of them died. On release from the cages, up to 40 per cent died within two or three days, unable to cope with the challenges of their new environment – all they knew how to do was swim around in circles inside an enclosure. A day or two of rough weather would result in thousands of them getting washed up on the riverbanks as, having been raised in cages, they did not know how to cope with choppy water and changes to the flow. Nor did they know how to recognise predators; when they encountered them, they did not swim away, but practically offered themselves up in sacrifice. Having been raised in captivity, they had not developed the skills that wild fish have to protect themselves from the other species that want to eat them.

* * *

At seventeen, I was still in school, but nearly ready to enter the adult world. I was very excited when some men came to the Tech and announced that they were looking for young lads who might be interested in going to Germany for a few months. Training was offered ahead of working at a factory near Shannon Airport – Hohenstein, which made filters and other pieces of equipment for aeroplanes. The work involved making wire-mesh and required specialised skills that were not available in Ireland at that time.

I put myself forward straight away and filled in an application form. Shortly after that, I did an interview with a Dr Rosenstock, a German who had been part of the occupying forces on the British Channel Islands during the Second World War. He had met an Irish woman and settled in Ireland after the war, and now Dr Rosenstock was employed finding staff for German companies setting up shop in Ireland. As the Limerick area already had an established relationship with Germany, because of the Shannon Scheme and because of Shannon Airport, it was an obvious place for German businesses looking to establish themselves in Ireland to consider.

A week or so after the interview, I got the good news: I had the job. Well, I was thrilled. This would be my first time overseas, and a fantastic opportunity to get on in life. I jumped at the chance, and Mam and Dad were delighted to see me getting a good start.

I felt on top of the world when I made my way to Shannon Airport and boarded the plane. It was an American airline. All the hostesses looked like beauty queens and had Yank accents. 'Where ya goin', Paddy?' they enquired sweetly. 'First time on a plane? Skeered? C'n ah git yew any-thin'?' They asked me questions about myself as they served me drinks and snacks, and told me that my accent was beautiful. I felt like a celebrity. As the plane took off, I looked out the window and watched my hometown getting smaller and smaller, until I couldn't see it any more. Between all the attention from the girls and the opportunity to get a good look at one of the most modern aircraft I had ever seen up close, a Pan-Am 707, it was one of the best days of my life. I remember it like it was yesterday.

I loved Germany, and most of all I loved the ready access to German airfields, where I could look at all the planes and imagine myself flying them. Just down the road from the factory where I was being trained, there was an airfield housing row after row of fighter jets. The local pubs were full of the pilots, and as I was now old enough to drink too – and getting increasingly fond of the beer, I might add – it was easy for me to fall into conversation with them. Most of them were English guys, and while some of them were delightful, others were less than friendly ('Fuck off, Paddy, no Micks here, innit?').

As I was still very young, the war seemed like history to me, but for people on the continent, memories of it were still very fresh. We were near the Dutch border, and I have rarely seen such hatred as that displayed by the Dutch people towards the Germans.

After six months in Germany, I returned to Ireland and a stint at the wire-mesh factory, where I did well. I had always been technically minded, and found it easy to use the equipment. There were opportunities for further training, but then the salmon season started. I weighed up the situation. I could stay in manufacturing and gradually get increasingly skilled so that I could move my way up the ranks at the factory, or I could earn what I could get during the winters and spend spring and summer in my favourite place, doing what I loved most. Even though the salmon fishery was not what it used to be, and despite Dad's wise counsel to stick with the factory, I decided on the latter. Like so many Coonagh men before me, I would go to London and work as hard as I could all winter long, freeing myself up for a summer on the river.

As my knowledge of the River Shannon had grown, so had my deep appreciation of the delicate balance of the ecosystem in which the salmon lived. Every fish, bird, mammal and plant species was engaged in a complex dance with each other, such that what impacted on one inevitably had a ripple effect on all the rest. Beyond the Shannon, the endless cycle of water – rain, springs, streams, rivers and oceans – was the metronome that set the rhythm for it all, as one season segued into the next and the years endlessly repeated.

All my life, Dad had told me not to become a fisherman, that there was no future in it. I heard what he was saying loud and clear, but I did not want it to be true. After all these years – thousands, really, back through my own Norman ancestors, to the time of the Vikings, and before that the Celts and all the other people who had lived on that same land and fished in those very waters – how could it be possible that it was all coming to an end? Had time run out just before my turn to take the helm? Why now? Why me? How could that be fair? How could it be right? I felt that I owed it to the generations of fishermen who had gone before me to keep the tradition and the knowledge alive. And so I did.

CHAPTER FOUR

The Old Ways and the Pull Back

I t was 1960, I was seventeen years old and, much as I loved tradition, I was also ready for adventure. The radio at home – the wireless – was my outlet. Mam and Dad wanted to listen to the news or sports, or a bit of Irish music, but I liked to tune into Radio Luxembourg, which had been entertaining young people all over Ireland and Britain since the 1930s. Here I heard the voices and music of young adults like me who lived in places that I envisioned as being much more exciting than County Limerick. I started to dream about seeing the world. Not about leaving Coonagh forever, mind you – just for long enough to get a taste of what other places had to offer, and long enough to put together sufficient cash to free me up for summers of fishing on the water. I knew that earning money abroad over the winter would make a summer fishing career on the Shannon financially viable.

In those days, vast numbers of young men and women emigrated to London for work. So many from my home area had left that this was a well-trodden path for me. Although a lot of the people in Coonagh – including Dad – held firm republican views, there was no ill feeling towards those who went to London, or indeed towards the English in general. Once they were not trying to rule Ireland, the general consensus was that the English were a fine people and generally quite easy to get along with. The only negative comments I ever heard levelled at those who emigrated to England was with reference to the few men who joined the British Army there. This was widely seen as a poor show, because although the money and opportunities were quite good in the army, as British soldiers they might be asked to participate in putting down the Irish people, or indeed other people who had never been given a fair deal.

As I had no intention of joining the army, Dad was happy enough to see me go. Mam and Dad knew that I needed more than was available to me at home, especially as it was getting harder and harder to make a decent living on the water. London was an exciting place then, full of opportunity and culturally vibrant. I looked forward to being part of what would become known as the Swinging Sixties.

Gabriel and I travelled up to Dublin on the train and got the mailboat from Dún Laoghaire to England. The whole boat was full of young Irish men and women, drinking beer and having fun on the way over. After another train ride across Wales and England, Gabriel and I found places to live in Camden Town, alongside thousands of other young Irish from all over the country. For the next few months, I lived in various digs, boarding houses and flat-shares all around Camden, picking up labouring and other heavy work. When I was not working hard, I was having fun in pubs like The Crown in Cricklewood, which was full to the rafters with Irish builders, plumbers, electricians, nurses and domestic staff every night of the week. I had never heard so many diverse Irish accents before I went to London. In Camden, there were Irish lads and girls from every part of the island, and it was easy to make friends. My pal Gabriel was better-looking than Elvis then. He could sing almost as well, and he smoked his fags with all the panache of a young Steve McQueen. Gabriel had the pick of the girls and, as neither of us was shy about striking up a conversation, we spent our evenings surrounded by other people.

Although London was very different to Coonagh, it was easy to settle in. I even had some family locally. My Uncle Joe, Dad's brother, had emigrated to London for work in the 1930s, had stayed on as the bombs fell in the 1940s, and was still there now. Joe was running one of the roughest pubs in the city, the Railway Station Hotel in Camden. He was tough enough to deal with the many fights that broke out there among the mainly Irish clientele. The Railway Station Hotel had lots of dances, frequented by tough Irish-speaking lads from Connemara and west Clare, who were up for a row if they thought someone was looking at them funny. I remembered the stories I had heard from Dad about the wild reputation of the Connemara lads who came down to Limerick to work on building Ardnacrusha.

Evenings often ended with the London bobbies in their silly tall hats pulling up outside. They would shove the rowdiest Irish fellas into their vehicles and bring them down to the station to sober up and calm down. The police, it must be said, were often very rough and rowdy themselves. While most of the English people I met were friendly and welcoming to the Irish, many police officers had strongly anti-Irish views and were quick to arrest the Irish, even when they were not doing much wrong. The police would frequently break up a fight outside an Irish pub with an entirely unreasonable degree of force, their truncheons inflicting way more damage than the row had in the first place. They seemed to get a kick out of it.

Although I was never in any trouble with the police, I did not miss them when I returned to Coonagh for the start of the fishing season. I was back again the next year, and thus established a migratory pattern that would last for years: the salmon-fishing season at home in Coonagh, followed by months of hard physical work and equally hard socialising in London. I would get work in factories, on building sites, wherever I could use my strength or technical ability to earn money during the winter months, and then I would drop it all and migrate to Coonagh for the salmon season, stepping back into my fishing gear and the family gandelow as though I had never been away at all. I felt comfortable and at home in both places.

Two years after my first jaunt there, I arrived back in London just in time for the Big Freeze of 1962–63, the coldest period ever recorded in the south of England. Temperatures stayed well under zero for weeks on end. There was heavy snowfall, rivers and ponds froze so hard that you could walk on them, and river boats were frozen into place. Even the salt water froze along some coastal areas. The English liked to think of themselves as a stoic and resilient people, and there was a great deal of invoking of the 'Blitz spirit' and talk about stiff upper lips and can-do attitudes. But as all the sports fixtures for the season were cancelled and drivers found themselves stuck under banks of snow, the stoicism started to waver. At the start, they had all been greeting each other with a cheerful 'Bit nippy, eh?' but now the mood was gloomy: 'Can't feel my blasted fingers; when will it end?' Fortunately, the London Underground was only minimally disrupted by the exceptionally wintry weather. People kept going to work and London stayed busy, although there was a lot of grumbling.

As the English like to say, it is an ill wind that blows no good. The Big Freeze was good news for me. The extremely cold snap meant that it was a good time to find work, because gas mains were breaking in the far-be-low-zero temperatures, and every day more of them needed repairs, all over London. It was hard, physical work, as they were buried four or five feet underground, but the pay was very good and the business owners affected by the breaks were generous, letting us workers into their premises to make tea and take our lunch breaks in a warm room. We also had fires in barrels outside to warm up around, and we paused work every now and again to hold our hands over the fire and let some blood back into our stiff fingers. As repairs were done around the clock, there were plenty of night shifts available, for which the pay was particularly generous. I was working very hard, and making more than twice as much as I would have back home doing a job like Dad's at the cement factory.

After repairing gas mains throughout that frigid winter, I found work in Euston railway station. Gabriel and I both worked there for a while, wearing the British Rail uniform, with its peaked cap. We moved trains between yards and platforms, directed freight trains and loaded trains heading for regional towns and cities with copies of the London newspapers, hot off the presses. We worked as porters, too, loading heavy chests and suitcases on their way to Southampton, where they and their owners would be decanted onto ships heading off all over the world. With a smile and a bit of friendly Irish banter, the tips could be enormous, because travel by ship was expensive in those days, and a lot of the people heading off on sea voyages were very well-heeled.

The 1960s was a time of huge economic growth in the city, and in the south of England generally. Watching the crowds coming and going from Euston, sometimes it seemed as though the entire world was flocking to London. London was five hundred miles from my home in Coonagh, and also light years ahead of it. London gave me the opportunity to meet people from a very wide variety of backgrounds. At that time, lots of young people from the British West Indies and from British colonies and former colonies in Africa were also moving to London for work and opportunity. In some ways, those countries were quite like Ireland then – educational levels were rising quite rapidly, but employment opportunities were not keeping pace, so bright young people were anxious to leave home and get a good start somewhere else. I got along very well with the ordinary working African guys, who were hard workers like the Irish, but not so well with the posh African students, who often came from big money at home and were used to having servants to do everything for them. Because the cost of living was so much higher in England than they were used to, they often had to do physical work for the first time in their lives to help with college expenses, but because they were used to being upper class and had very high opinions of themselves, they were not always very good at it or enthusiastic about it.

I was having such an enjoyable time in London in those first few years that I gave very little thought to my friends and family. I wrote very few letters to my parents, but when I thought of it, I used a public phone booth to ring O'Halloran's shop in Coonagh and leave a message for my mother, just to let her know that I was okay.

But while I loved my time over there, as winter turned into spring, my thoughts invariably returned to the Shannon. The fishing season was starting there. I knew that the remaining fishermen of Coonagh would be putting the finishing touches to their gear and gandelows, and I wanted to be with them. The bright lights of London started to dull and I got a sort of an ache inside that I knew would only go away when I put my two feet on the riverbank in Coonagh and smelled the Shannon air. In the year of the Big Freeze, I went back in March, and it was cold in Ireland too. A thick frost lay on the ground most nights and ice clung to the reeds on either side of the river, discomfiting the waterbirds. The day after I arrived, I was out in my gandelow on the Shannon, casting my nets for the salmon, with a flask of tea and a bottle of stout to keep me warm.

London was good to me, I have to say. It welcomed me when I came, looked after me while I was there, and never held a grudge when I left in the spring. I joined a football club, Priory United, that played out of Kilburn on Sundays, and made some English friends who sustained me every year through the winter months. One day, someone handed me a brochure for an airshow in Welwyn Garden City. Welwyn is a planned community that was built before the Second World War, about twenty miles north of London, and events were often held there for people day-tripping from the city. I remember looking at the brochure and thinking of the small planes I had watched fly over my home in Coonagh for as long as I could remember. I decided to go.

It was already extremely exciting to walk around the airfield and look at all of the diverse types of aircraft, but when I got the opportunity to actually get into one, my excitement was off the Richter scale. Tiger Moths are small biplanes that were first built by the de Havilland Aircraft Company in the 1930s. They had been used by the Royal Air Force to train military pilots and even take part in military exercises, but by the 1960s, the RAF had moved on and sold a lot of the Tiger Moths to private users. The woman pilot smiled at me as I climbed on board. She told me to buckle in and handed me a pair of goggles. 'Are you ready, Paddy?' she asked as the plane started to move down the runway. 'There's no way out of it now! The only way is up!' I was almost too excited to answer her. I think I managed a nod.

I had been on a plane before, when I took the Pan-Am to and from Germany, but being up in the air in this two-seater was a completely different feeling. After the initial excitement about being in the Pam-Am had worn off, it had not really been that different to being on a bus. Soaring above Welwyn, with the green English countryside, little English villages and the greyish sprawl and yellowish smog of London's suburbs spread out beneath me, was completely different. It was as close as a human could get to flying – really flying, like a bird. As I gazed down at the landscape below – the tidy little English villages, the sprawl of the suburbs and beyond that the smoky haze over London – I wished that I was looking down on my own homeplace instead of someone else's. I felt a brief pang of homesickness.

By the time we landed, I was hooked. From then on, I watched out for every airshow and went to them all. I started to dream of one day having a little plane of my own, although for now I certainly could not afford one – I spent money almost as quickly as I earned it, mostly on going out and having a fun time.

I was in my mid-twenties now, and many of the people I knew of my age were settling into their adult lives. I realised that if I decided to stay in London, I could do very well. It was a land of opportunity then, and I was a quick learner who could have fitted into all sorts of jobs. London offered me a thousand more ways to get on in life than Coonagh. I could have stayed there and put down roots. I can easily imagine the alternative life I might have led: getting further training in a field like engineering, and perhaps working in an aeroplane factory, or sticking with a company like British Rail and moving my way up through the ranks.

If I had chosen a path like that, eventually, like so many of the up-and-coming Irish, I would have moved out of digs and flats in Camden into the middle classes and a tidy semi-d in an English suburb, where every man's house is his castle and the boundary between his garden and the neighbour's is jealously guarded. I could have watched the locals playing cricket on the green and perhaps even joined in the odd time. Maybe started picking up a bit of the accent. All of that. A life that a lot of people might consider enviable.

But every year, as winter turned into spring, I would find it harder and harder to stay. I knew that back home the hawthorn buds were starting to open, the brown river waters starting to get warmer, and the salmon embarking on their epic journeys from the mysterious depths of the North Atlantic to the familiar flow of the Shannon. My body would be in London then, taking me to and from work every day and going through the motions, but my mind would be back in Coonagh, thinking about the nets and other equipment needed for the season. I would be imagining how it would feel when, for the first time that year, I pushed the gandelow out into the Shannon and stepped aboard, the water rippling around the prow as we heaved off from the bank, the pale yellow light of early spring filtering through the reeds on either side of the river.

Sometimes I would try to delay the pull back to the Shannon by going down to the Thames to look at the water and the boats there. There was all sorts of boat traffic on the Thames in those days: freight, passenger and tourist barges, and more. There was good money to be made, and with my experience I could easily have picked up work on one of the river boats, but somehow I knew that working on a different river from my own would be worse than not working on any at all.

The Thames could not compare to the Shannon in any case. The Thames was absolutely filthy in those days, and had been for a long time. The last

Thames salmon had been caught in 1833, with the river described around the mid-nineteenth century as 'a common sewer'.[96] Before the Second World War, efforts had been underway to reduce the amount of sewage released into the water, but the London bombings of the war had seriously damaged the sewerage system. In the 1960s, a huge percentage of untreated London sewage was still going straight into the river. On a warm day, and especially at low tide when the mudflats were exposed, it stank. It was so dirty that where it flowed through London, and from London to the sea, the Thames was considered essentially biologically dead. Very few forms of life could survive in it, and there were essentially no fish. As far as I was concerned, a river without fish in it was no river at all.

At the weekends, my friends and I would go to Regent's Park, where we could rent a rowing boat at the boating pond. It was fun, but a poor substitute for a Shannon gandelow. There were always plenty of little boats bobbing around – a mum and dad taking their kids out, or young fellas trying to impress their girlfriends. They all stilled their oars, stopped talking and stared when two or three boatloads of us sturdy Shannon lads took to the water and raced each other across the lake, getting up to such high speeds that the prows of the pleasure boats made little waves as they surged through the shallow water, frightening the overfed city ducks.

I had been a Shannon fisherman since childhood and no matter how hard I tried, I could not reinvent myself as someone else. At some point every spring, my mind would return to the Shannon, to the graceful motion of the net through the air when it was cast off the side, the sky shining through its diamond apertures; to the ebb and flow of the river tide; to the flash of a salmon's bright scales through the water when the sun glinted off it. My migrations from London back to Coonagh in time for the salmon fishing season still mirrored those of the fish. I chose to overlook the fact that, as Dad said, there was no future in fishing. Year after year, I gave my notice at whatever job I was working in and, like the salmon, migrated back to the waters where I had been born.

I loved everything about the Shannon – the movement of the tide, the waterbirds, the reflection of the reeds on the water's flat brown surface. I loved, too, the knowledge that I was following the path of generations of fishermen, all the way back to God knows when, each passing down its knowledge to the next. Most of all, I loved how, when I was fishing, I was my own man, my own boss. Nobody was telling me what to do; I would succeed or fail on my own terms. Every fisherman, young or old, is a captain in his own right.

But disappearing fast was the old-style fishing with hemp nets, which gave the fisherman a decent living, and the Atlantic wild salmon a fair chance. And another traditional source of income from the river was also disappearing: the tough work of cutting reeds with a sickle ahead of putting them in sheaves for the thatchers. This was little needed now – as the traditional houses were gradually replaced with new, slate-roofed homes, the demand for reeds for thatch dropped.

Winter was the season for harvesting reeds, and while thatching was much less common than before, the money in harvesting reeds was still okay – not enough to provide an income in itself, but certainly quite a lucrative side hustle. The gandelow slipped handily in and out and around the little inlets in the muddy banks, and was a firm base for the piles of reeds as they accumulated.

The repetitive motions of the sickle – Austrian-made, wooden-handled, serrated-edged, the finest quality we could buy – were almost meditative, the work physically demanding but rewarding. Time would pass quickly as I cut on, lost in my own thoughts until the friendly voice of another reed-cutter called out a greeting, breaking the trance, or the gandelow filled and it was time to go home. After a hard day's work, the gandelow would be slung even lower in the water than usual. Back on shore, the reeds would be bundled into ricks and prepared for the thatchers.

As the 1960s proceeded, there were some winters when I considered staying in Coonagh and forgetting about London for that year. But in the evenings, as the dark drew in and we all pulled our chairs closer to the fire, I would think of the bright neon lights of Piccadilly Circus and the crowded dancehalls of Camden. They would be packed to the rafters with excited young Irish people – the girls' mouths shiny with lipstick, the boys' cigarettes at jaunty angles and hair slick with Brylcreem, and everyone's eyes glittering with excitement – and once again I would want to be gone. Soon I would be saying goodbye again – a hug and a kiss for Mam, a firm handshake for Dad – and getting the train to the Dún Laoghaire mailboat. For years, that is how it was.

CHAPTER FIVE

Motoring On

As the hydroelectric plant at Ardnacrusha moved into its fourth decade of operation, there was growing awareness of the challenges it posed to the fish. When I was small, there had seemed to be almost no limit to the wild salmon. The older people could remember a time when there had been many more than I ever saw, as things had already changed dramatically before I was born. By the 1960s, the numbers of salmon were still in steep decline, while demand for the delicious fish stayed high.

Now, attempts were made to control the catch by issuing licences. Most small-scale fishermen had no option but to follow the law – as Dad had always done because, as I have said, he could see the sense of it. But there was a lot of money to be made, and those in positions of greater power often overfished with impunity. The politicians did not seem to care. There was talk of vested interests influencing them, and possibly encouraging them to turn a blind eye to some of the more influential individuals involved in the fisheries. The State appeared to be in opposition to the interests of the environment.

At the same time, pollution was becoming increasingly evident in the Shannon. It was not nearly as bad as the Thames, but it was getting steadily worse. The fishermen's nets now often picked up condoms and other rubbish discharged into the Shannon by the sewerage and drainage systems of the city. Contraception was, of course, illegal in Ireland, and had been since the Criminal Law Amendment Act of 1935, so everyone blamed the condoms on the sailors whose ships docked in Limerick.

Some said that the sailors should not even be let into the country, with their immoral, heathen ways. At that time, you would still often hear the older people describing England – where I came of age as a young adult – as a pagan country, with the people up to all sorts of immorality. The truth was that everything that was happening in England was happening in Ireland too. The only difference was that in Ireland nobody talked about it openly.

Condom use would not be formally legalised in Ireland until 1975, but ask anyone who was fishing the Shannon back in the 1960s and they will tell you just how widespread it was. Either those foreign sailors were using admirably prodigious numbers of condoms, and should have been complimented for their stamina, or half of Ireland was using them too, even though few people were prepared to discuss it.

Also by the mid-1960s, growing numbers of Irish women were taking contraceptive pills on prescription for medical reasons – a convenient loophole around the strict Irish legislation of those days – and artificial hormones were entering the water in escalating quantities too. As these were invisible to the naked eye, we would not realise for many years what was happening, and did not understand for years after that what they were doing to the environment.

The city was a major polluter with the detritus of ordinary urban living, but farming and industry were also big problems, which were rapidly getting worse. Many farmers with properties along the Shannon used to throw dead animals into the river to get rid of them. Fairly often, out on the water, I would encounter a dead cow, sheep or pig floating down with the current, its belly massively swollen with the gases of decomposition. Sometimes its four legs would be bolt upright into the air, the hooves pointing accusingly at the sky above. Farm animals that died of disease were supposed to be carefully buried, far from any source of fresh water, but digging a hole big enough and deep enough was a lot of work, and not everyone could be bothered with it. The river seemed an easy place to dispose of things – anything unwanted would simply drift away. But of course, these cadavers would become tangled in the reeds somewhere and then gradually rot down, picked over by scavengers, and disintegrate. The skull would be the last thing to fall apart, and you would often see one at the side of the river, a tangle of reeds pushing up through an empty eye socket.

Rising acidification of the waters in which salmon lived was another problem. The Meteorological Service had been measuring the acidity of rain in Ireland since 1948. This measure rose steadily throughout the 1960s – and would continue to do so afterwards – due to industrialisation. This was not just in Ireland, but also elsewhere, as once the atmosphere has been polluted, the wind can carry the pollution anywhere. Higher levels of acidity in river water compromise the viability of salmon eggs, and are also thought to contribute to mutations in embryos and just-hatched alevins, making them less likely to survive and thrive.[97]

Clearly, the huge cultural and social changes that my generation was living through all had complex impacts on the environment that few, if any, of us understood at the time. Throughout the 1960s, Ireland became almost completely electrified, with just a very few homes in isolated areas without power. Having lagged behind the rest of western Europe for centuries, Ireland was also industrialising rapidly, with all sorts of factories opening up in both urban and relatively rural areas. Shannon was a prime spot for development, with its international airport and a local workforce that was increasingly well-educated and ready to work for less money than in many other countries.

Despite rising levels of education, the 1950s had been a period of severe economic stagnation and rising emigration levels in Ireland. It was clear that the protectionist policies of the previous decades were holding back the development of industry. By the late 1950s, however – shortly before I went to London for the first time – Seán Lemass, the Minister for Industry and Commerce, was to the fore in promoting outward-looking policies. By the late 1950s, amid very high rates of emigration, the Shannon Free Airport Development Authority was established. From 1959, it worked to attract foreign multinationals to the area. It offered pre-made factories, tax exemptions and grants, an enthusiastic local workforce and a convenient location beside an international airport, from where goods could be transported around the world.

The first pre-built factory at Shannon was opened on 4 April 1960 by Erskine Childers, then Minister for Transport and Power. By the mid-1960s, a lot of the people I had grown up with in Coonagh, including some of my own siblings, were working in factories like Rippen, Pink, Sony, Lana Knit, Progress, SPS, Hohenstein and Spee. They manufactured pianos, fabric-marking machines, radios, fabrics, precision fasteners, plastic buttons, and the wire mesh that I had been trained to make in Germany a few years before.

Most of these factory workers were earning more money than their parents could ever have dreamed of. They were living in comfortable, modern bungalows with all the mod cons then available – fridges, washing machines, electric ovens and more – and they were going on holidays to seaside towns or Butlins, or sometimes even Spain, which seemed to have only recently been invented. Their children – in most cases, thanks to growing access to contraception and gradually changing social mores, fewer of them than their parents had raised – were going to finish secondary school at the very minimum, and many of them would go on to university and acquire professional qualifications.

In 1967, educational standards in Ireland took another huge leap forward when Limerick man Donogh O'Malley, Fianna Fáil Minister for Education and a former mayor of Limerick, introduced free second-level education, as well as free buses to transport children in rural areas to secondary schools. Not all of his fellow government ministers were happy about these changes, which cost a lot of money, but the Irish public was delighted and the numbers attending secondary school soared. O'Malley died in 1968, so he never saw how much his brave decision to change Irish educational policy for the better helped to transform our country, stem the tide of emigration and lay the foundations for prosperity. I remember a time when poverty – serious poverty – was widespread in the outskirts of Limerick. The new educational environment and the new jobs coming on stream had extraordinary effects, utterly transforming people's lives.

While most people were still going to Mass and felt close to their faith, their relationship with the Church was changing too. My parents' generation and the generations before them had often been quite apprehensive of the local parish priest, who had enormous power in the community. If he called you out from the altar for some misdeed, you were in serious trouble, and your own friends might start avoiding you in case they got tarred with the same brush.

When I was a child, the Church was very down on communism, and Mass invariably ended with three Hail Marys and three Our Fathers for the conversion of Russia. Now, with the changes resulting from the Second Vatican Council coming down the line from the mid-1960s, people were increasingly thinking for themselves. Even if they were not attracted to the idea of communism per se, they were now wondering just what was so bad about working people standing up for their rights.

Changing views on religion were not so much about walking away from their faith, but more about embracing it on their own terms. The missions I remember from my childhood were becoming a thing of the past, as most people no longer wanted to spend their hard-earned free time hearing about what terrible sinners they were and how the flames of hell were waiting for them. Mass went into English, and we were getting a new generation of priests, who were much more inclined to talk about how God was love and less about hellfire and damnation. Sometimes they would even whip out a guitar and sing a religious ditty in a folksy style, which was very confusing for the older parishioners, who often missed the Latin Mass.

Not long before, people had been almost afraid to discuss religion beyond repeating what they heard at church, because they were scared of saying the wrong thing and getting called out from the altar. Now sometimes you would hear someone say of a friend, 'Sure, that fella doesn't believe in God at all!' While they might be saying it disapprovingly, it really did not matter the way it used to, and would not stop them from palling around with him. You might even hear someone opining that, in all likelihood, the

communists were probably mostly just ordinary men and women like ourselves, and that maybe we should try to get our own house in order before
casting aspersions on others' affairs. Mind you, the Shannon fishermen –
even the ones among us with atheistic leanings – maintained their firm
belief in the protective powers of a vial of holy water, and not a one of us
would have gone out fishing without it.

We'd had RTÉ television in Ireland since 1963, and a lot of us had been
watching English television before that. My own family had purchased our
first TV around 1960, a marvellous device that would have been unimaginable just fifteen years earlier. Before everyone started getting televisions,
people had gathered in each other's homes to read the newspaper, or read it
to one another, and discuss the news. Even those older people who had relatively little formal education were extremely interested in the wider world,
and had well-informed and usually very strong opinions about everything.
The television put an end to all of that. Now all the talk was about *The Late
Late Show* and its handsome young presenter Gay Byrne, and who had said
what to whom. Mam and Dad, who had always liked to be informed about
current affairs, were enthralled.

Many of the factories that seemed to be providing hard workers with
bright futures ran open sewers and pipes straight into the Shannon, carrying
chemicals, human waste and more. Some pipes carried substances so nox-
ious that they could only be flushed out during times of heavy rain, as otherwise workers in the factory would have been at risk of passing out, or even
dying, from inhaling the poisonous fumes. The mouths of such pipes were
often invisible from the land, but I had an unobstructed view of them from
the river. At low tide, the stench would have to be smelled to be believed.
Where the effluent came into contact with the riverbank, all vegetation died,

leaving muddy, oily, ugly black wounds on the otherwise green slopes. Common waterbirds such as the heron, which hunted for fish from the banks, stayed well away, as they quickly learned that there was nothing to eat there. As it was harder for them to feed, their numbers dropped rapidly.

We fishermen talked about the growing levels of pollution that we were seeing, especially when it impacted directly on us, such as when rubbish got tangled in a net. But, like most people then, we had no idea how bad it already was, let alone how bad it was going to get. We had no real understanding of the numerous ways in which we ourselves were unwittingly contributing to the problem. Most fishermen needed to have more than one job to support their families – Dad had always worked in the cement factory, for example. There was much more industry in the area now, and many locals worked in the same factories and plants that tipped all of their human and industrial waste straight into the Shannon. There was a near-consensus that the downsides of development were a price worth paying to have good jobs locally, so that the younger generation would not feel forced to emigrate.

Despite rising employment opportunities and incomes, emigration was still a feature of Coonagh life. A lot of the other lads Gabriel and I had grown up with had emigrated permanently. Many of them ended up meeting women in far-flung parts of America and Australia and settling down long distances from home, building lives very different to the ones they had known as children.

Industrialisation was a way to stem this flight of the brightest and the best, and so we all embraced it. We did not yet understand how badly the high and growing levels of pollution were damaging the entire ecosystem of the Shannon and the countryside it ran through. That knowledge was yet to come.

At this time, the fishermen's gear was undergoing dramatic change. Plastics were replacing everything that had previously been made of materials that degraded quite rapidly. While this was happening in every sector, from agriculture to industry and everything in between, the impacts on fishing were huge and immediately felt. The new equipment was much more effective than traditional gear, and the difference it made to how we worked was dramatic. By the mid-1960s, hardly anyone was fishing with hemp nets, and all of our equipment was made with nylon and other plastics. This change had taken place very quickly. While a few people had been using nylon nets from the mid-1950s – those who could afford it and were most open to innovation – most fishermen adopted their use over just a few years in the early 1960s. Whereas before, fishermen had seen themselves as hunters, and the salmon had had a fighting chance, with only a very small proportion of them taken as catch, the new equipment could sweep a river and take in everything. And, of course, when nets and other equipment got lost, they became indestructible detritus that got tangled in weeds, killed wildlife and interfered with the movement of fish and other animals. To make matters even worse, the new and improved equipment somewhat disguised the devastation taking place beneath the surface of the river – because the nylon nets were more effective than the hemp ones, they temporarily hid the plummeting numbers of wild salmon.

By now, the salmon hatchery at Parteen Weir had been operating for several years, and it was generally hailed as a remarkable success. Certainly, the ESB was now releasing enormous numbers of smolts into the river every year. Between 1966 and 1969, about 200,000 one-year-old smolts were released from the hatchery into the Shannon annually. The hope was that the baby fish would participate in the normal salmon migration pattern and return in a year or two. The ESB stated that this would ensure a healthy stock of fish for all those exploiting the salmon in the Shannon, including the approximately two hundred and fifty people then employed in net-fishing in the estuary area.[98]

Most of the fishermen working on the Shannon at that time, including me, were delighted with the hatchery. The idea of rearing young salmon in a safe environment and then releasing them into the wild to repopulate the river sounded like a wonderful idea. We all hoped it would result in the recovery of the Shannon fisheries and the preservation of our traditional way of life. But the ranched smolts – and the larger salmon that some of them became – were not quite the same as the native fish, in all sorts of ways. This would become increasingly apparent over the coming years.

At this time, outboard motors were adopted en masse by the river-fishing community; I bought my first on hire purchase in 1961, and did not look back. By the mid-1960s, Yamaha – already well known for its motorcycles and pianos – was the big brand. Their outboard motors were relatively light and affordable, and could be adapted for use on most smaller fishing boats. They could be attached to a traditional wooden gandelow with just a few small adjustments to the boat, providing the motor with a firm structural base to bolt to.

Fishing was much easier with an outboard motor. In fact, it was no longer necessary to have a crew of three or four, because now you could do the same amount of work, or even more, with just two. Before, the gandelows had been bigger, to carry three or even four men, but now they were narrower, built for a pair of fisherman, with just enough space for a reasonably slender third when the weather was bad and an extra hand was required.

Since outboard motors had arrived on the market, boatbuilders made their vessels with stronger, more robust transoms – the wide, flat part on the outside of the vessel's stern – of hardwoods like oak that could bear the weight of a motor. Fishermen strengthened the transom in older boats with a piece of angle iron or other material – it needed to be strong enough to attach the outboard motor and flat enough that it would not catch on the net. The motor made it very easy to travel considerable distances and allowed fishermen to completely compensate for the drift of the river, which can easily carry a gandelow a mile or so, sometimes completely out of a fish-rich section of the river. While this previously required the crew to row arduously back, with an outboard motor they could return to their original spot in minutes with almost no effort at all. Thanks to the outboard motor, crews had much more time to spend actually fishing, which increased their catch, even though the numbers of salmon in the river were continuing to dwindle. In this way, outboard motors also contributed to a lack of awareness of what was really going on.

The fishing community in Coonagh largely split in two, along generational lines, on the topic of outboard motors. The younger fishermen, like me, were all strongly in favour of them, because they were relatively inexpensive, available through hire purchase, quite easy to operate and really cut down on the physical work of fishing at a time when it was increasingly difficult to put together a crew. The older guys, in their fifties, sixties and beyond, were often quite suspicious of them. Some of them were even hostile to them: 'Oh Jaysus,' I remember one local fisherman saying. 'Go away wit' that aul' yoke! I'll throw the feckin' thing overboard if you don't take it out of the bloody boat. What are you carryin' that weight around for all day, only for nothin'?'

An outboard motor could be fickle sometimes and tricky to start. You often needed to give it a few goes – while everyone else shouted advice, which was often contradictory – before the motor would finally splutter and kick into life.

More women were now joining crews than before. This was partly because outboard motors largely negated any need for upper-body strength, but also because it was ever harder to put together all-men crews. Women also tended to be highly skilled at handling nets, which was a meticulous, tricky job. The older men were sometimes sceptical about working with women and girls, as they had been about the adoption of outboard motors, but the younger ones generally had no problem with it. Getting the job done, and done well, was all that mattered.

Just a few years after outboard motors started arriving in Coonagh, criticisms of them faded and practically everyone was using one. Anyone who did not was soon left behind. They made life much easier and they also made the river a much noisier place. Before, you might hear the slip-slop-splash of oars going in and out of the water, and the sound of fishermen chatting among themselves – and occasionally letting out a roar at one another. Now, there were fewer boats, with smaller crews and outboard motors. You did not hear oars very much anymore and there was less chatting. Every time someone started up their outboard motor, it sounded like a motorbike revving to life. The heavy smells of petrol and oil now hung over our mooring spots, and occasional leaks from the engines of the outboard motors left oily rainbow puddles on the surface of the water there.

Friendship between fishermen had a particular shape on the river. One of the reasons why it was difficult for me to say goodbye to the Shannon fisheries was the thought of losing the strange closeness that develops between crew members on a boat. As fishing is such dangerous work, and crews are quite small in the salmon fisheries, everyone's life on a crew is literally in each other's hands. You have to have absolute faith and trust in the people you are with to keep you all safe. You all have to do the right thing at the right time, and never take any shortcuts, or someone could die. Even when everyone does everything right, accidents can still happen, and then you have to believe that your crew members will be able to pull you back on board and bring you home in one piece. It can be easy to underestimate risk – I have done so myself. One time I took to the water after drinking too much and I went overboard. Thankfully, I came up at the side of the boat, and no harm was done.

With the complete integration of the outboard motors into our work, it was now common for just two men to work together as one, each anticipating what the other was about to do. Together, they let out the maximum allowed length of net – a hundred and thirty-five yards – at just the right angle to capture the salmon. Conversations were mostly about the tide, because everything the fishermen did depended on it, and about the presence or absence of good numbers of fish. We would talk about other things too, of course, almost anything: women, politics, the cost of living, hopes and dreams for the future. On a calm night, you might be on the water for hours after the nets had gone out. Sitting there in the dark, listening to the water lap against the low sides of the gandelow and unable to see one another's faces without turning on a torch, it seemed possible to say or ask anything in a way that it never was on dry land.

Gabriel, who was so handsome he could have made a fortune in Hollywood if he had wanted to, had come home from London. He married a lovely girl and settled in Coonagh, where he continued to fish as he and his wife started a family. Now he was supporting his wife and family largely with his earnings from the fishery. As children, Gabriel and I had loved games of make-believe, cowboys and Indians and all the rest of it. As young adults out on the water, we mostly talked about fish, tides and the weather, but somehow in the gaps between those words we also spoke about everything else. By the time we were twenty-seven years old, in 1970, Gabriel and I were very experienced fishermen. We knew each other so well that, on the water, we could predict each other's every move.

One evening, Gabriel was out fishing on the Shannon, close to Bunratty River, near the castle of the same name, with another friend. Having taken a short break ashore for a meal, they were about to resume fishing and had just got on board, when he tripped, fell overboard and hit the back of his head on a rock. He got up and was swimming around – despite his heavy clothing and waders – but although his friend called out to him, he said nothing back. His friend and others who had witnessed the scene tried to save him, but before they could reach him, Gabriel sank beneath the surface. By the time he was recovered from the water, he was gone. I thank God that I was not there that day, and I have nothing but pity for the friends who were. There must be nothing worse than helplessly seeing a companion die.

What happened that day was nobody's fault, but having nobody to blame did not make it any easier. The people of Coonagh accepted the dangers of the work they did – all the fishermen still carried holy water with them, to help keep them safe – but this loss was particularly hard, for Gabriel's family and for the whole community. For me, who had lost such a close friend, it was devastating. At the afters of his funeral, I drank far too much to blot out what I was feeling. This loss was almost more than I could bear.

I have been asked in the past why this terrible tragedy did not put me off fishing forever. I do not know the answer, and I can see how it might have done. But I can tell you that, far from driving me away from the water that had taken the life of my friend, it only made me love it more. Now, when I took to the Shannon, I felt Gabriel's absence in the boat the way I had once felt his presence, as if his silent ghost was pressing the gandelow lower in the water and sharing with me my hopes and concerns for the day's fishing.

Beyond Gabriel, it sometimes seemed as though I was accompanied by a silent army of all the past Shannon fishermen whose lives had been taken by the river, or by the naval warfare in foreign seas in which so many participated. I honoured them all in the lowering and raising of my nets, and held imaginary conversations with them about the situation I observed: how the salmon I was catching were getting ever fewer, and how the water I worked seemed to contain so much less life than it had when we were kids.

When Gabriel and I were little boys, leppin' excitedly up and down on the riverbank as the men came back, people had come down with carts and wagons to take away the fish. Now you could carry a full day's catch in just a small hand-basket.

CHAPTER SIX

A Crisis Mounts

In the late 1960s and early '70s, the Irish government pumped money and energy into projects intended to restock Irish fresh waters with salmon. During that time, although the number of wild fish continued to plummet, catches were still relatively good, because the new nets were so much more effective than the old, traditional ones – despite falling numbers, people were actually landing more fish. Those who fished the Shannon in the 1970s remember some very large catches, up to a hundred salmon per day,[99] and they were making very good money. It was easy for fishermen and the State authorities to assume – or to pretend – that everything was fine, and most people did. In fact, by this time, if you looked closely, there was already enough data to show that ranched salmon were a severe threat to wild salmon.[100] The good catches were hiding a much more dismal reality.

With each year that passed, there were many fewer wild salmon, and now almost all of the fish pulled in were ranched. These ranched fish were much smaller than the wild salmon had been before. In the early twentieth century – before the construction of Ardnacrusha – the average size of a spring salmon caught on the Shannon was over twenty pounds. This is more than twice as big as a good-sized newborn human infant and provides a large amount of meat. Now a fish that size was considered rare – interesting enough to get into the newspaper – and the general trend was that they were getting progressively smaller with each year that passed. Younger people did not even remember what the fish had looked like before.

In Coonagh, and in fishing communities the length and breadth of the country, some of the fishermen tried to raise the alarm, to explain to the authorities what they were seeing on the water. But their evidence was dismissed as anecdotal. Their deep knowledge was ignored, because it had been acquired through experience rather than university, and because it was inconvenient.

Dad passed away in 1974, when I was thirty-two and long before I was ready to say goodbye to him. He was only sixty-four years old at the time of his death; cancer took him from us years before he should have gone. He had always been a strong, vigorous and positive man, and it was very difficult for all of us – but of course especially for Mam – to see him getting progressively smaller and weaker towards the end. He died about six months after his initial diagnosis. I was glad that I was able to be with him in Coonagh for most of his illness, at a time when I was still migrating to and from London.

While Dad had been supportive of all his children's choices in life, he had advised us for years to abandon any idea of making a living from the Shannon. He said that there was no longer a future in fishing. He had seen for himself how, since he had arrived in the area in the 1920s, the numbers of fish had plummeted and their behaviours had changed. 'You'd be better off getting yourself a steady job,' Dad had said. 'There are no fish there now.' I remember hearing him say that and not wanting it to be true, but knowing at the same time that it was, because I had seen it for myself. Even in the final weeks and months of his life, Dad was thinking of his children's futures and giving this advice.

Above: The awesome structure of Ardnacrusha under construction in 1927.

Below: A team at the hard manual work involved in the project.

Patsy aged about eighteen in his British Rail porter's uniform, when he worked at Euston Station in London.

Patsy aged about twenty on his bike in Coonagh, County Limerick.

Patsy's mother, Nora, in her fifties.

Jimmy Ryan, Patsy, Thomas O'Halloran, Billy Grimes and Paddy Davis in London. All of them were from fishing families in County Limerick.

Around 1961, Coonagh briefly reverted to its true identity as an island when the Shannon River broke its banks and filled the tidal flood plains. William Grimes, Jimmy Ryan, Tom Davis, and Betty, Frances and Mary Cronin.

Brother and sister Joe Keegan and Kathleen O'Neill and their aunt Norah Peril with the house painted in the Clare colours.

Patsy piling thatching reeds on the Ennis Road.

Zoology students Tanya Power and friend, from NUI Galway, with their nets and other equipment, working as fishing crew members with Patsy in the early 2000s.

Patsy and plane in the Channel Islands, on the way to France to celebrate a former student being awarded her pilot's licence.

Around 2010, at Hegarty's Boatyard in Cork. Patsy at the restoration of a famous boat belonging to Conor O'Brien, who built it in 1925 for service on the Falkland Islands.

Protesting in Dublin in the early 2000s, highlighting the level of wastage taking place in fisheries at sea. At that time, about ninety per cent of fish caught and wasted were juveniles, far from fully grown.

Above: Outside the Dáil. From left: Brendan Price, Patsy, John Daly. Only one TD came over to take a look.

Below: A press conference in Buswell's Hotel in Dublin, showing the shocking wastage involved in bycatches.

Slieve League, Donegal, in the early 2000s: Patsy with Noel Carr, who leads the Federation of Irish Salmon and Sea Trout Anglers' Association.

A leap of faith: An Atlantic salmon in an Irish river, answering the call of the wild to reach its spawning grounds, and play a now-critical part in the survival of the species.

We laid Dad to rest in Mount Saint Lawrence Cemetery in Limerick City, where we have a family plot. I dedicated my next fishing trip on the Shannon to him. I sat there in my gandelow, a light rain falling on my head and shoulders, thinking about how he had taught me everything I knew about the river and its inhabitants, how Dad had lovingly guided my hands when I was a little boy casting the drift net for the first time, how proud he had been when I killed my first salmon and brought it home to Mam. Eventually I could not bear his absence anymore, so I brought the boat back to shore and went home. It was a tough time.

Dad's death forced me to look at the future, but also made me feel closer to the past. He had always been very interested in history and the various revolutions and wars that had taken place in Ireland, up to and including conflicts that he and his family had themselves been involved in. Around this time, affordable metal detectors came onto the market, and I bought one. Exploring a local site where there had once been a castle – one of the many of the Earls of Thomond from Bunratty – I found artifacts associated with bullet manufacture back in the 1600s: ball-shaped bullets in a wooden case that was still somewhat intact. The bullets had been put into the case when they were red-hot, and you could still see scorch marks on the wood, angry reminders of a troubled time in Irish history. I wished I could have shown them to Dad. I think he would have liked the idea of the men who made them, many years before, wanting to defend Coonagh from intruders. Coonagh, and the Shannon flowing through it, needed protecting again now.

I had been fishing since childhood, and now I was approaching my mid-thirties – still young, but old enough to have seen things changing too. In my approximately two decades of working on the water, I had witnessed the number of salmon decline dramatically and the general health of the river deteriorate. It was getting harder and harder to ignore what was going on. There was some, but not enough, talk about the challenges facing the environment – the river environment in particular. On top of Ardnacrusha and its associated infrastructure contributing to the salmon's troubles for decades, the situation with plastic pollution was getting worse and worse, not just in the Shannon and the surrounding areas, but everywhere.

Retail in Ireland at that time was switching rapidly from small, specialist shops to big supermarkets, where you could get everything under one roof. A few years before, housewives had done their grocery shopping every day, getting the ingredients they needed to feed their families. Many rural – and even some urban and suburban – families also produced quite a lot of the food they needed themselves, growing their own potatoes, cabbages and onions, and often keeping a few hens and a pig for eggs and meat.

Now more families had cars, and it was becoming customary to do a big weekly shop for heavily packaged goods. Ever-larger numbers of products were coming wrapped in copious quantities of plastic, while customers took all their shopping home in disposable plastic bags. Discarded plastic bags were already becoming a feature of the landscape in the 1960s. By the mid-1970s, substantial numbers of them were making their way into the Shannon. At low tide, plastic bags fluttered in the breeze from the lower branches of the trees lining the riverbanks. A bag that got well stuck in a tree might stay there for years until a particularly heavy storm blew it away. Plastics clung to the reeds on either side of the river, where they were a problem for nesting birds. They filled with water and sank below the surface, where they were a problem for fish. They could also become entangled in fishing nets, dragging them down with the weight of the water they contained and making it much harder to pull the nets on board.

More and more of the rubbish that made its way from Limerick's city streets into the Shannon was plastic too. Detritus from the city had always entered the river, with the sewers spewing filth from big pipes, but at least up to now, most of it had been biodegradable materials that eventually rotted away. Plastic lasts forever. Farms contributed plastic as well, in the form of discarded fertiliser bags and other packaging. It was suddenly everywhere, like a sort of mould growing on almost every surface – except, unlike mould, you could not just rub it off. After a while, I think a lot of people kind of stopped noticing it, or simply accepted it as part of the landscape or – like the pipes dripping fetid waste into the river – a reasonable price to pay for the progress we were all enjoying.

Agricultural policies being promoted by the government at that time were part of the problem. In 1972, 83 per cent of the population had voted in favour of Ireland joining the European Economic Community (EEC), and there was a big push throughout the 1970s to modernise Irish agriculture, which was seen as not reaching its potential. At the time, many new agricultural technologies were coming onto the market and young farmers were increasingly likely to have attended agricultural college or university. They came home with a lot of big ideas about the latest scientific approaches to working the land. Growing numbers of farmers were adopting new, much more industrial methods of producing food. These methods resulted in much higher levels of waste, in much denser concentrations, and a lot of it seemed to end up in the river.

Often, from my vantage point in the gandelow, I could see and smell the dark-brown run-off from silage, which was increasingly replacing hay as a feed for animals over the winter. Silage is made by cutting grass while it is still green, mixing it with molasses, compacting it in a silage pit and allowing it to ferment. This malodorous mixture does not go musty or rot, which can happen to hay in a bad year, and it is a reliable source of food for farm animals during the winter months. Silage removes a lot of uncertainty and anxiety around how to keep a dairy herd fed during the long winter when the grass is not growing.

By the mid-1970s, there seemed to be concrete silage pits everywhere, typically covered in big sheets of thick, sturdy black plastic, generally weighed down with old tractor tyres. Around Limerick, the silage pits were often located close enough to the water that most of the run-off found its way into the Shannon. Effluent from silage pits is corrosive, and its high-nutrient content pollutes water and can lead to excessive bacterial growth and algal blooms that threaten the integrity of the river ecosystem. The plastic covering it is heavy and strong, but with repeated use it breaks down, shreds and enters the environment too. Silage was a great friend to the farmer, but not to the fisherman, and certainly not to the fish.

The decline in the number of hay meadows also impacted negatively on mammal, bird and insect species, because now grasses that would previously have been allowed to mature, flower and seed were being cut at an earlier stage to make silage. Silage, then, contributed to a decline in species diversity both in the water and in the meadows alongside it. It was all horribly visible from a little boat in the middle of the Shannon, but I had no idea what, if anything, could be done about it.

Dairy farming, always a backbone of the Irish economy, was also getting progressively more industrial. This was partly because, with innovations in animal husbandry such as modern mechanised milking machines and dairy sheds, it was easier than before for farmers to maintain very large numbers of cows. Dairy had been a central plank of the rural economy for countless generations, but now Ireland was becoming a very major exporter of milk products, from butter to baby formula. More and more farmers had enormous herds, and the sight of huge milk tankers making their way along small country roads was increasingly common. So too was the sight of a milk tanker pulled up alongside a quiet patch of the Shannon, being scoured out directly into the river. In fresh water, milk is an appalling pollutant, which kills everything it meets. So are the chemical rinses that people were using to wash the tankers out with.

The fact that farmers and dairies displayed little to no discretion about using the Shannon as a sewer speaks loudly of the fact that most people simply did not understand how human factors were damaging the natural environment. They were not ashamed of what they were doing, because they did not know they should have been. People complained at length when they got stuck behind a milk tanker on a narrow lane and could not pass, but most said nothing about tankers being washed out into the Shannon, as they simply did not realise that it was a problem.

Industries were getting larger and more polluting too. Because both the government and the ordinary people were so anxious for Ireland to develop and industrialise, to provide solid jobs for willing workers, there was little appetite for ensuring that even basic precautions were taken to minimise harm to the environment. I remember one factory opening up and spewing such toxic substances into the Fergus River, a tributary of the Shannon, that the entire flatfish population of the area – sole, plaice, dab – died out within a couple of years. When I was younger, we had switched to fishing for flatfish once the salmon season ended, both for our own consumption and for the fishmongers in town. There was little point in doing that now, as there were so few flatfish left. Knowing how dirty the water was in the places where I had previously caught flatfish for the table, I did not particularly want to eat it anyway.

As someone who felt more at home on the Shannon than in my own house, I was increasingly aware of how precarious the health of the river and of the salmon and other species that lived there was. Hazards were everywhere: fish too aggressively, and the breeding population would be too small to regenerate; remove predators from the environment, and species whose numbers were normally kept under control would have a population explosion, threatening their competitors.

A salmon population that was already in steep decline because of the hydroelectric plant was now further stressed by toxicants and rubbish in the water, and was also being overfished at sea. Until the mid-1970s, most of the fish caught in Ireland were caught in rivers. From the 1960s, this had started to change, with increasing numbers caught at sea. By about 1975, most fish caught in Ireland were caught in the sea. Previously, sea fishermen had used small vessels and had landed relatively modest catches, selling them directly to customers or to local fishmongers. The marine economy ran parallel to similar small fishing enterprises in rivers and estuaries. Increasingly, the new generation of sea fishermen were using large trawlers with enormous nets, capable of landing vast quantities of fish. They now supplied factories, which processed the fish in several ways, preparing them for the huge supermarkets springing up everywhere as well as for the export market.

From the point of view of the Shannon fishermen, a big problem here was that, although we were fishing in different environments, we were often after the same fish, and the small river boats could never compete with the monster trawlers. In nature, the salmon's migratory route takes them from their natal river to the Atlantic, where – as we have seen – they spend one or two years roaming, foraging, and growing, often spending a lot of time in the icy waters of Greenland. Knowing how to forage is key to the survival of the wild salmon. When they are ready to spawn, they return to their rivers once more.

In my childhood, and for thousands of years before that, salmon caught in rivers were a staple of ordinary people's diets on both sides of the North Atlantic, and comparatively few were ever caught at sea. Now, most of the salmon born in Ireland were being captured as they travelled through the Atlantic, or down the Irish coast as they journeyed back towards their natal rivers. Already, few salmon could reach their spawning grounds in dammed rivers like the Shannon. Now, most of them did not even get as far as the mouths of their home rivers.

There had always been occasional conflicts between fishermen, when one felt that another had encroached on his patch – especially after a few pints had been taken in the evening following a hard day's work. Now that the fish were harder to catch, these conflicts became more frequent and led to more ill feeling than before. Coonagh started to change. A fishing community that had always pulled in unison, it began to be pushed apart. Cooperative fishing had always been the glue that kept the people of Coonagh together. Now, if we still wanted to be a community, we had to find something else.

Partly because of my love of soccer and partly because I wanted to do something for the next generation of little boys growing up in Coonagh, to help them maintain a community they could be proud of, I helped to set up a football club here. We had loads of skilful players, but because we did not have our own club, they all played away from home. A few like-minded fellas and myself held a public meeting to assess interest and soon a team was formed. I watched the young lads run around the field, full of enthusiasm for the game and without a care in the world, or an inkling of how social and technological changes in Ireland were impacting on their families. I couldn't help but think of my own childhood and the endless hours of fun that my friends and I had enjoyed in the self-same fields. Our fathers had all fished the river. Only a few of theirs did. Would any of them even grow up to know how?

* * *

At first, salmon farming seemed like a satisfactory solution to the problem of the disappearing Atlantic wild salmon and, possibly, to the associated problems of the Shannon fishermen. There had been quite successful farms for rainbow trout in Ireland since the late 1950s, but it is much easier to raise rainbow trout in captivity, because they can be reared for their whole life cycle in fresh water, and they deal relatively well with the crowded conditions of a farm. So many generations of rainbow trout have been raised this way that they can be regarded almost as a domesticated species. By 1970, Irish trout farms were producing about eighty-four tonnes of trout every year,[101] and the public was getting used to the idea of eating farmed fish. Surely salmon could be farmed too?

The first serious attempts to breed salmon artificially took place in the nineteenth century, and by the end of that century hatcheries were in operation on both sides of the Atlantic.[102] While salmon farming is complex, because salmon need salt water for much of their life cycle and are a migratory species, places like Norway and the Faroes were far ahead of Ireland in this area, and they were spreading a very positive message about the results they were seeing. From the 1960s, organisations like the Mowi Company in Bergen described healthy, happy salmon that could be grown and bred in captivity relatively easily. They were satisfying the public's appetite, while leaving most of the wild salmon to thrive in their natural environment. By 1972, Mowi was producing two hundred tons of salmon, and planning to expand its business considerably.[103] It all sounded like a win-win proposition.

The first large, modern salmon farms started to appear in Ireland in the mid-1970s. Salmon farming would be a growth industry in the decades to follow, supported at every level of the State, from the humblest county councillor to the Taoiseach himself, regardless of which political party was in power at any given time. From 1974, the ESB – which had a responsibility for the welfare of salmon, badly impacted by hydroelectric plants – provided smolts to salmon farms from the hatchery at Parteen in Birdhill. They initially sent them to a salmon farm in Carna in Galway, where the fish were raised in large cages in the Atlantic.[104]

Because the 1935 Shannon Electricity Act made it clear that the Electricity Supply Board should prioritise generating electricity over the welfare of the wild fish, they seemed to feel off the hook regarding providing a viable natural environment. The Act states that '… subject and without prejudice to, the primary function of maintaining, working, and developing the Shannon hydro-electric works … the Board shall have and perform the duty of managing, conducting, and preserving the Shannon fisheries under and in accordance with this Act.' The careful wording of this clause gives the superficial impression that the ESB would take responsibility for the welfare of the salmon and other species. However, on a more careful reading, '… subject to … the primary function …' clearly states that all other things could and should be sacrificed to the cause of generating electricity. This applied as salmon farms were rolled out just as it had in the preceding decades.

By the late 1970s, entrepreneurs from Ireland and overseas were establishing more salmon farms along the Irish Atlantic coast to cater for demand, stocking them with smolts from hatcheries, including the ESB's own. People were getting used to buying whatever they wanted to eat, at any time of the year, in large supermarkets. The whole idea of seasonal food was going out the window. At first, fishermen from places like Coonagh had given the new salmon farms very little thought. Most of us assumed that they would just create another product for the market, and that they would not really impact on the wild fisheries. If anything, some regarded them as potentially a good thing, believing the official government line that if salmon farms provided the supermarkets with cheap, farmed fish, there would be less strain on the wild population. These could then be fished at a sustainable level, using the age-old methods that we all knew so well, and marketed as a luxury product. In the initial stages of salmon farming in Ireland, I myself felt quite positive about the fish farms. I hoped that farmed salmon would relieve pressure on the wild population and might contribute towards the preservation of the traditional Shannon fisheries and my community's way of life.

The salmon farms were a natural extension of the hatcheries. The idea was that, instead of releasing artificially reared salmon and hoping that they would behave like wild salmon, hatchery fish could be raised in a contained environment until they were adult fish, ready for the market. Certain types of fish have been raised in ponds for centuries – since the Middle

Ages, monks across Europe often farmed species like perch and roach – but farming salmon is more challenging, as they are migratory and so confinement in an enclosed space is stressful for them. However, the public appetite for salmon was always very high, and there was huge money to be made. The hatcheries' original stated mission of repopulating the natural environment with salmon that would travel their normal migratory routes seemed to have been sidelined.

The hatcheries, of course, needed eggs, and they got many of them from the wild fish that were already struggling so badly to complete their life cycle. The poor salmon would arrive at the ESB's weirs, hoping to complete the final leg of their journey and deposit eggs in their redds. Now, instead of being allowed to pass, many of them were scooped up and physically emptied of their precious eggs and sperm, which would be used in a controlled environment to create a new generation.

The process of removing eggs and sperm from salmon that are ready to breed is a brutally simple one. The fish are removed from the water at the weir and placed in a pen. Then, one by one, they are simply squeezed out, in a process that I am sure is extremely uncomfortable for the fish. The females are checked periodically to see when they are ready to ovulate. When the eggs are ready to be released, gentle pressure will result in a few coming from inside her body, and the fishery workers know they can now 'strip' the eggs. To do this, the female is held slightly on the side with her tail pointing down, and the worker applies pressure along her body towards her egg vent, emptying the eggs into a receptacle underneath. The sperm, or milt, is removed from the adult males by a similar process. Both types of gamete remain viable outside the fishes' bodies long enough for fertilisation to take place artificially. The eggs can now develop in a controlled environment, and can then be used to populate the hatchery, which in turn will supply the fish farm.

The adult wild fish, thus stripped of their capacity to reproduce naturally as the logical conclusion of their migratory journey, can be returned to the wild, in the hope that they will re-enter their natural cycle. Exhausted, and presumably highly stressed as a result of the stripping process, most will die rather than return to the Atlantic to take part in another cycle. While the mortality rate of spawning salmon is extremely high in any case, with large numbers perishing naturally in the process, one can expect to see even higher rates of mortality among such stressed fish.

Salmon fish farms need a particular sort of environment. Whereas the young fish grow from eggs to the smolt stage in fresh water – such as at the hatchery at the Parteen Weir – to get to the next stage, they need to move to salt water. In Ireland in the 1970s and '80s, salmon farms were increasingly located in our Atlantic waters. They consisted of huge, cylindrical cages in the water, each containing an extremely concentrated population of fish. This is a very stressful and unhealthy environment for a creature that evolved to travel large distances and to live a largely solitary life. For any creature, living with chronic stress is of itself unhealthy and damaging. Chronically stressed animals are particularly susceptible to disease, so whenever any sort of disease or parasite entered the crowded fish enclosures, of course it spread like wildfire. The losses were almost unimaginable. Someone farming sheep or cattle whose animals' death rate was even five per cent of what the salmon fisheries were experiencing would have been closed down by the authorities. Yet State bodies blithely accepted that very few of the young salmon delivered to the farms would mature and become adults big enough to make it onto supermarket shelves.

While salmon farms met market demands for fresh salmon, it made an already dreadful situation worse for the wild ones. It gradually emerged that the positive news we had heard about salmon farms in other countries was no more than propaganda, and that in fact these farms were already damaging the fragile salmon ecosystems in their areas and beyond.

As a challenging situation turned into an environmental disaster, the government oversaw a big publicity drive for farmed salmon, with the intention of promoting it as a staple food for ordinary families. Advertising campaigns informed consumers that farmed fish was a healthy option for them, and urged parents to feed their children more fish. It was implied that farmed fish was just as good – or indeed even better – than wild fish. The campaigns were an enormous success. Soon salmon farmers were making so much money that some trout farms also started producing salmon smolts to provide to salmon farms off the Atlantic coast.

Few of the consumers who bought pre-packaged salmon steaks in the shiny new supermarkets had any concept about the reality of the industry, and the quality of the product. The truth was that the farmed fish they were buying were often diseased, so that sometimes the flesh was not the normal, characteristic salmon-pink, but a nasty greyish-white. A wild salmon's pink flesh results from them eating creatures like shrimp and krill. One way of ensuring that the farmed flesh looked approximately normal was by feeding the salmon special food, with added carotenoids, in the final stages of their lives. These carotenoids could either be from natural ingredients, like ground-up crustaceans, or from synthetic forms created in a lab. Buyers, such as supermarket chains, were shown a colour-card with a range of options, and could choose the exact shade of salmon flesh they wanted. This strategic feeding of salmon with particular foods allowed the meat from sickly salmon to pass for the real thing on the shelf of a chilled compartment. For someone like me, who had been reared with fresh wild salmon, and knew what it was supposed to taste like, the farmed stuff was almost inedible.

For years, hatcheries at Parteen Weir and elsewhere had been releasing fish into the wild that were poorly equipped to survive. Now the farmed salmon, which were often unwell and riddled with parasites, escaped into wild waters too, bringing disease, infestations and their poorly adapted behaviours with them. Sea lice became much more of a problem than before.

Sea lice (*Lepeophtheirus salmonis* and members of the *Caligus* genus) start off as free-swimming larvae, but when they encounter salmon, they settle onto them as parasites. They attach firmly to their skin and feed directly from them, causing physical damage and stress to the salmon, and compromising their ability to grow and thrive. Sea lice are natural creatures and have their role in the wild ecosystem, but with hundreds of thousands of salmon crammed into a small area in a fish farm, once sea lice enter a farmed population, they spread rapidly and compromise the health of the fish. Some of these escape and then roam the Atlantic with much higher than normal levels of infestation, transmitting lice to wild fish in areas where salmon congregate. Head lice spread like wildfire among young children in primary schools, because children spend many hours in an enclosed environment, in close physical contact with one another. You can imagine how swiftly sea lice spreads in a fish-farm environment, in which salmon are packed so closely together they can barely move.

The name 'sea lice' is a bit of a misnomer. The lice that roam the heads of children in primary schools are very small, and do not really cause much of a health risk beyond the scratching, but sea lice are completely different. They attach themselves like leeches, in their dozens. They bore holes into the salmon and essentially devour them. A fully grown salmon can survive with a small number attached, though the lice will affect their health, but if there are too many, they can die.

At this time, it was becoming increasingly clear that government policy was not to support small-scale fishing by traditional communities. It was getting harder and harder for the families of Coonagh, who had been supporting themselves with their fishery for countless generations, to afford licences for the fairly modest quantities of fish they expected to catch. By the late 1970s, at Thomond Weir, downstream from the Ardnacrusha hydroelectric plant, an area where local fishermen had once easily landed twenty thousand salmon every year, they now only caught a few hundred. That same year, the ESB permanently closed its own commercial fishery at Thomond Weir, because there were no longer any fish to catch there. But licences appeared to be plentiful for those fishing the Atlantic with big boats and deep pockets. Most of the fishermen of the Shannon had never earned more than a modest income. Now, fifty-odd years after the building of Ardnacrusha, it was extremely galling for them to see wealthy, well-connected fishermen with large, modern trawlers apparently given free rein to catch as many fish as they wanted from the Atlantic waters off the Irish coast.

* * *

As I moved through my thirties, I continued my seasonal migrations from London to Coonagh and back again. Ireland was changing quickly, and

London was changing too. London had been a boom town in the 1960s, with jobs for everybody and plenty of opportunities to get ahead. By the mid-1970s, the atmosphere was much less optimistic. Immigrants and migrants seemed less welcome, and the atmosphere in public places was edgier. Even the music young people were listening to was getting angrier, as the mop-top hairstyles made fashionable by The Beatles gave way to the aggressive, artificially coloured spikes of the punk rockers.

The Irish community in London was changing as well. When I had started migrating, Camden had been filled with Irish faces and Irish accents. It had been a home from home for us all, where we knew we would always be able to find like-minded people who knew where we were coming from. Now the Irish were dispersing, and there was no longer such a focal point for the Irish community. It was still relatively easy for me to find work, but it was getting more difficult to have fun.

In 1978, along came England's infamous Winter of Discontent, with strikes frequently grinding the whole country to a halt. But I was young and strong and I could still pick up well-paid work in London. I earned enough money to give it all up in the spring and return to Coonagh for the fishing season.

Every year, fewer of my peers joined me on the river. Most of them now worked in factories near Shannon Airport. Some of them were very happy with their jobs and a new way of life that was completely unlike their parents', but others would have loved to follow in their forebears' footsteps and spend the fishing season in their gandelows, like me. The problem was that my generation increasingly just did not have a choice.

At home, people often asked me why I did not want to get a decent job at one of the factories in Shannon. It was a reasonable question, and it was certainly something that I had considered. In my late teens, I had quite enjoyed my stint at the wire-mesh factory. But having grown up in Coonagh, the son of a fisherman and of a very independent-minded woman, I hated the thought of the factory hierarchy. I didn't want to be told what to do, what time I had to come in and when I could take a break for my lunch and my cup of tea. Out on the water, I was king of my own gandelow and I could work as much or as little as I wanted. As a fisherman, I knew that every penny I made was the result of my own hard work, and that if I did not go to work I would not make anything. That is what I wanted for myself, and I also wanted it as an option for other people of my age, and for the next generation coming up.

I could see that the Irish government did not really care about me or anyone else who made their living from the Shannon, so I decided to see what I could do to make things better for us. Initially at a local level, I became involved in grass-roots organisations that strove to represent the smaller fishermen and give them a place at the table. From 1977, I became a representative of the Shannon Net Fishermen's Association – which was open to everyone engaged in net fishing in the River Shannon and its tributaries. The activism I was involved in would become a huge part of my life for years to come, and is still one of the main reasons why I get up in the morning. In the beginning, my main interest was in promoting the rights of small fishermen – people like my dad, the other men I knew from Coonagh, and of course myself. I felt we needed to stand up for our rights, as it was very clear that nobody else was going to.

I became ever-more aware that the interests of small fishermen and of the natural environment are, in fact, one and the same. Without healthy rivers and seas, the species that populate them living in a natural balance with one another, there is no future at all. All around the North Atlantic region, the habitat of the Atlantic wild salmon, others were coming to the same realisation. By now, conservationists and governments had started talking about the fact that, while other migratory marine species such as tuna and whales had relatively robust legal protections, the same was not true of the salmon.

Modest efforts to protect salmon in the region had begun in 1972, when the US/Danish Atlantic Salmon Agreement laid out a plan for the phasing-out of salmon fishing in Greenland. This idea was, of course, fiercely resisted by Greenlanders, who had access to salmon migrating from all over the Atlantic region to feed there.[105] Greenland gained home rule over their own domestic affairs from May 1979,[106] and with greater independence came great risk for the salmon.

I am sure that home rule for the Greenlanders was brilliant news for them in many ways – and as the son of a republican, I am naturally in favour of self-determination for all peoples – but it was terrible news for the salmon. As it happens, the most important feeding ground for Atlantic wild salmon is off the coast of Greenland. Once the sea-fishers from all over the Atlantic region cottoned on to this, they headed straight there and started to net some enormous catches. As they did, river communities on both sides of the Atlantic observed a dramatic fall in the already depleted population of salmon returning to their natal rivers.

Greenland had automatically joined the EEC when Denmark became a member in 1973; now its membership was in doubt, and along with it whatever limited protections fish were given under European law. The complexity of devising a system to protect a migratory fish that moves across such a vast territory became clear: once at sea, does any nation have a claim over a particular fish? But, complex or not, it was now obvious that nobody's government was doing nearly enough to protect the salmon, the fisheries in general, or indeed the entire marine and riverine environment.

CHAPTER SEVEN

Stark Reality

Like most of the men of Coonagh – and also some of the women – I was fond of the drink. The drink was almost a religion in Coonagh when I was younger. Every special occasion, from the birth of a child to the funeral of a member of the community, was marked with copious consumption of alcohol. Coonagh funerals, in particular, were legendary in the Limerick area for their wildness. Stories were often told of visitors from elsewhere mistaking a funeral gathering for a wedding party, such was the level of merriment on display.

As a young man, I drank both to celebrate and to drown my sorrows. I never drank so much that it stopped me from working or getting on with my life, but I can freely admit that a lot of the money I earned went down the drain. I had started drinking more heavily after Gabriel's drowning, when we were both aged twenty-seven. I was as drunk as an owl, as they say, at his funeral. Gradually, it seemed more and more normal and natural to use alcohol to numb my feelings on those days when things were not going well, as well as to order a pint the minute I had something to celebrate.

I woke up one morning in 1980, crawled out of bed and opened the window to have a cigarette. As I stood there, leaning on the window ledge, puffing on my fag, I realised that it was time to stop drinking. It was the last day of the fishing season, and I had been working my arse off over the past few months. I had made a good few quid, and I had drunk almost all of it. After all that arduous work, there was very little of my hard-earned money left. In the harsh light of day, with a headache from drink starting to pound behind my eyes, I self-diagnosed myself as a functional alcoholic. It's time to stop all that, I told myself firmly. That's enough. I looked at the cigarette pinched between my nicotine-stained fingers, and decided that while I was at it, I might as well stop smoking, too. I flicked the butt into the long grass outside the window, hearing it hiss in the damp as it went out. From now on, I decided, I would devote all my extra money to flying planes instead of drinking pints, maybe even get a little plane of my own when I had saved up enough. It is dangerous enough to be drunk in charge of a boat; being drunk in charge of a plane would be a death sentence.

I have not had a drop since, and I have flown all over Europe in a small plane. Instead of pouring most of my money down the drain, I started throwing it all up into the sky. I have no regrets. Every pound I spent on flying was money well invested, and many of the happiest moments of my life have been among the clouds.

I had been fascinated with air transport since early childhood when planes had often flown over our house on their way to and from Shannon Airport. As the Limerick Flying Club was located in Coonagh, I knew from an early age that flying was something anyone could do, provided they were prepared to do all the required lessons and spend a bit of money on it. Flying has a close historical link with the boating fraternity too – to this day, many nautical terms are also applied to aircraft – so it seemed appropriate that the club is on the banks of the Shannon.

As a matter of fact, in 1948, Ireland's first international air rally was held by the Shannon Aero Club at Coonagh.[107] I was five or six years old at the time and, like all the other children in Coonagh, I was fascinated by the light aircraft and by the impossibly glamorous pilots, who seemed almost like superhuman beings. For months afterwards, we all argued about which pilots were the best and played games inspired by the small planes and the aerial acrobatics we had seen. We made our own small planes by hammering nails through sticks and set up little 'airfields' outside our houses with these toy planes carefully lined up.

My fascination with flying had only grown when I learned a little more about it, visiting air shows in the Greater London area. Back in Coonagh, one of the members of the Flying Club with whom I was friendly – Anne, an enthusiast of light aircraft – asked me to teach her how to row, so that she could explore the Shannon and see the local wildlife for herself. In return, she paid for my first flying lesson. It would be one of those breakthrough times, when I realised something important about myself. As a child, the day I killed my first salmon, I realised that I was a fisherman. As a man, the day I flew a plane for the first time, I realised that I was a pilot, too. It was as simple as that.

My first experience behind the controls of an aircraft was provided by a German count, John Sierstorpff, who had settled in Ireland. I had been up in light aircraft before, as a passenger, but taking the controls in my own hands was a dream come true. The wind was high and the little plane was violently buffeted from side to side as we rose above Coonagh. Once we were up, we swung around and flew to Adare, in County Limerick. I was concentrating very hard on what the good count was saying so that I could commit it all to memory, but I was still able to look down at the landscape below us. From the near distance of a light aircraft's trajectory, I literally had a bird's-eye view of my home and of almost the entire route of the beautiful River Shannon as it carved its way through the Irish landscape to the sea near Limerick.

It is difficult to describe the emotions that washed over me that day. I imagine Neil Armstrong must have felt something similar when he stood on the moon for the first time, looking back at Earth. I am not an overly religious man, but for me the experience was almost a spiritual one, an awakening of the senses that – even though I was in the sky because of aeronautical technology – made me feel closer to nature than ever before.

When we landed, John told me that he had nearly decided against taking me up, because it was so windy. 'Have you been put off for life?' he asked. When I assured him that quite the opposite was the case, we agreed that I must have been put on this Earth to fly. I took out my membership in the Flying Club that very day, and signed up for all the lessons I would need to get my own licence.

I have been flying ever since, and every single time I experience all of the same emotions as I did that first day. For me there is no freedom as absolute, as liberating, as purely joyful as flying by myself, looking from my perch in the sky at the landscape below me, having left my worries behind on the land. Up there, I know that my life is in my own hands. For me, heaven would be staying in the sky forever, all by myself, where I feel at peace with knowing how fragile I am, and also knowing how strong I can be.

* * *

While I was embracing a fresh start in my life, all around me it was becoming abundantly clear that there was no fresh start for the Shannon or for the village of Coonagh in the foreseeable future. The village was utterly transformed. It had never been a wealthy place, but it had always been a hive of activity, with men and boys fishing salmon in season and cutting reeds for thatch in the winter months, and all the residents kept busy in their various ways, always in tune with the ebb and flow of the river tide and the movement of the seasons. For countless generations, Coonagh had been a tight-knit fishing community characterised by cooperation. As children, we had all felt free to run in and out of each other's homes, and no fisherman had ever struggled to put together a crew. Most of us boys growing up had assumed that we would follow our fathers into the business of fishing and harvesting reeds, and that we in turn would settle locally and, if we had families, raise them there.

Now the population was aging, as young families moved out and on. Some of them would no doubt have gone away even without the decline in the fisheries, but I know that there were plenty who would have loved to stay and to watch their children grow up playing in the same green fields, with the same deep love of the Shannon waters that had been so important to their families for so long.

Even though I now had over three decades of salmon-fishing under my belt, and knew the Shannon as well or better than anybody, by now my own catch was almost all fish that had originated in the ESB hatchery in Birdhill. Some of the fishermen and almost all of the authorities pointed to the fact that catches coming in were quite large. That was often true – but those large catches were extremely deceptive, because they were almost entirely composed of ranched fish, and those were so unsuccessful at surviving and returning to spawn that the population was unsustainable.[108] Even those salmon that did return to their native river did not always know where to go to find a suitable place to spawn. Because they had been born in the hatchery, they headed there. They wouldn't even try to make it further upstream to the shallow gravel beds where conditions were ideal for the females to make their redds. At this point, the ESB would retrieve a certain number of the unfortunate fish that had managed to return to the hatchery. They were used to create a new generation of ranched fish lacking the instincts needed to survive and reproduce without human intervention.

With each generation born and raised to the smolt stage in captivity, natural selection and the evolutionary process were compromised further. When these same fish were released into the wild, they were not well-adapted to the wild environment, with behavioural problems that contributed to higher than normal levels of mortality, such as failing to recognise and move away from predators. Research has shown that using ranched fish to double the population of salmon in a particular river reduced productivity – the rate of successful reproduction – by half, resulting in no overall benefit at all.[109]

On 10 December 1982 – decades too late, almost six after work began on the Ardnacrusha power station – the United Nations Convention on the Law of the Sea was adopted. This is a series of rules governing how the resources of the world's oceans and seas should be treated. This was the most comprehensive and progressive environmental law of any modern international agreement to date,[110] and included an obligation for signatories

to take measures to protect fragile ecosystems and the habitats of endangered species. The objectives of the Convention were, among other things, to establish principles for responsible fishing and for the conservation of fisheries. With respect to anadromous fish, such as the Atlantic salmon, the Convention states that where they migrate into or through the waters of a state other than the state where they were born, the two nations in question should cooperate in conserving and managing the stocks. Both nations where the fish originated, and all those that exploited them, were to form regional organisations to devise and implement means of preserving them.

A year later, in 1983, the Convention for the Conservation of Salmon in the North Atlantic Ocean followed. The parties to the convention were Canada, Denmark (representing the interests of the Faroe Islands and Greenland), the EEC (of which the United Kingdom was then a member), Norway, the Russian Federation and the United States of America. The year after that, in 1984, the North Atlantic Salmon Conservation Organisation (NASCO) was formed, with the objective of conserving, restoring and managing stocks of Atlantic wild salmon by means of international cooperation and continuing scientific research.

The Atlantic wild salmon now had a certain amount of protection in law, but the hatchery salmon were not wild, and therefore were not subject to protection. This meant that fish raised in hatcheries could legally be confined in fish farms rather than released into the wild. Ranched fish, born in hatcheries and then released to follow the salmon's natural migratory routes, were also not protected by the legislation. We were now looking at a migratory salmon population that was almost entirely ranched, with vanishingly few fish that could be considered truly wild, and returns that were diminishing year on year.

Another issue was that a huge disparity was opening up between the numbers of fish caught at sea and those caught in rivers. The hatcheries were flooding the rivers downstream with artificially raised smolts. While many of the smolts were consumed by the usual range of natural predators, reasonable numbers of them were reaching the Atlantic and spending time there, eating and growing.

Coastal fishermen, who were as familiar with the salmon's movements in coastal waters as the Shannon fishermen were with their movements in fresh water, were able to catch good numbers of salmon up and down the western seaboard. Fishermen from places like Greenland and the Faroes, in whose waters the salmon fed, were catching enormous numbers of these fish, and even places like Donegal, in the northwest of Ireland, were reporting large catches. Innovative technologies, like the use of sonar for finding fish, were making it easier for well-equipped boats to figure out where the fish were, and to capture them quickly and efficiently. Those which survived capture, predation and disease returned to their places of origin. With each year that passed, fewer of these fish came back to the Shannon to spawn, and of those few, only a miniscule number managed to make their way upstream to the spawning grounds.

By now, I noted that about 30 per cent of the fish I caught bore the marks of nets – damage to their skin caused by escaping through the filaments of a net. Fish that had escaped from nets at sea were often reproductively compromised as a result of being crushed. They would never lay or fertilise eggs, so even if they did manage to come home, their journey would be wasted. While I knew then how bad things were getting in the Shannon region, I still did not quite understand the enormity of the situation. In fact, the exact same scenario was playing out all across the North Atlantic region. Ireland was actively destroying its own stock of wild salmon, and so was everybody else. It was an environmental disaster.

In Ireland, the ESB and the government continued to avert their eyes from their own roles in this disaster. I am not sure who said it first, but quite quickly a narrative emerged that the Atlantic seal was contributing to the disaster facing the wild salmon. This story was soon filling the airwaves, and sea-fishermen started campaigning for a seal cull. They claimed that if the numbers of seal were vastly reduced, the numbers of salmon would rebound, and then there would be more than enough for the human predators. They spoke in hugely emotive terms, attempting to paint the seals as fearsome creatures that were almost literally taking the food out of the mouths of Irish children, and this at a time of high unemployment, when many working families were struggling.

Some fishermen started killing seals, by leaving poisoned fish as bait, shooting them and trapping them. Injured and dying seals began to wash up on beaches and shorelines in numbers never before seen. The killers ignored the fact that seals and salmon, together with multiple other species, had coexisted in a harmonious ecosystem forever. The seal – just like the salmon – is a species fundamental to the Irish environment and deeply embedded in the collective Irish identity, in the form of legends, lore and iconography. We will never improve the fate of one species by simply eliminating or reducing the numbers of another. In October 1982, I spoke out for the first time, in a letter to *The Irish Times*. I wrote that it was painfully clear that the wild salmon population was in steep decline, and that the cause for this situation was certainly more complex than a lot of people maintained. I pointed out that the seals were an easy target, because they could not respond to accusations that they were solely responsible for the excessive extraction of salmon from the ecosystem. The number of seals had rebounded to a degree since reaching a low point in the early 1900s – in particular grey seals, which became the first mammals to be protected under modern legislation when the British government enacted the Grey Seals Protection Act of 1914. However, there were still far fewer seals than there were people, and they were much less rapacious, as they only took what they themselves needed to eat. They were also a protected species in Ireland, under the Irish Wildlife Act of 1976 and the EEC's Marine Mammal Protection Act of 1972. They were not nearly as destructive as was being claimed. In fact, while seals often did attempt to make their way into fishermen's nets to take fish, very often they themselves became entangled in them and drowned, or escaped with a net tangled around their neck or flippers, only to die of starvation shortly afterwards as a result. Far from being the main threat to the salmon, vast numbers of seals were dying as a direct result of modern fishing techniques and technology.

Things were bad for salmon, and other species, in the Shannon area – but this problem was not just about the Shannon, and not just about Ireland. In fact, the environmental, social and political factors that were conspiring to destroy the Atlantic wild salmon were systemic. All of the countries, and all of the political systems, of the region seemed to be colluding to wipe the species off the face of the Earth – perhaps mostly through inertia.

The authorities in Ireland, as elsewhere, had been aware of the crisis facing the wild salmon for some time. Their numbers had been plummeting since the first hydroelectric stations were built, and as contamination of river waters grew progressively worse, along with the huge levels of overfishing in the Atlantic, so did the situation facing the salmon. It was intensely frustrating, for someone from a Shannon fishing background, that the last people any of the so-called experts listened to were the small fishermen. The fishermen of the Shannon were often patronised and dismissed, on the grounds that we didn't have scientific training. The men making millions from their huge fishing trawlers had the economic weight and influence to dominate the conversations.

Of course, inland fishermen knew more about the river habitat than anyone – our livelihoods depended on it, and we were often descended from generations of fishing folk, with profound levels of knowledge that had been passed down over the years. We could see for ourselves how the numbers of salmon were dropping even further, while the net marks on the few we did catch hinted at the absolute piracy that was happening at sea.

Quotas and legislation intended to minimise damage to the environment were not effectively enforced. Some people were making fortunes in the process. Poaching salmon had become an enormous source of income, and it seemed that the managing authorities were very good at looking the other way, even though most fisheries officers were doing their best, and often working in dangerous circumstances.

By 1983, my colleagues in the Shannon Estuary Net-Fishermen's Association estimated that illegal salmon exports were worth about forty million pounds, at a time when traditional fishing communities like Coonagh were struggling badly. We called on the then Minister for Fisheries, Paddy O'Toole, to withdraw forty extra licences issued to sea fishermen in Kerry, because it was clear that there was widespread abuse of them, with massive overfishing of salmon taking place at sea during the hours of darkness.

Many sea fishermen were also openly using nylon monofilament nets that were 3000 yards long, or twice the maximum length permitted by law.[111] In the summer of that year, there were violent clashes between naval and garda personnel and salmon fishermen at various points along the Atlantic coast, when the former attempted to police the latter.[112]

In the autumn of 1983, Minister O'Toole introduced a ban on drift netting at the mouth of the Shannon. This was supposed to prevent excessive fishing of the run of salmon heading into the Shannon and up towards the spawning grounds. But the reality was that most of the salmon that should have been coming to spawn had already been captured at sea, while most of those that did manage to make it as far as the mouth of the Shannon might go on to reach the Parteen Weir at Birdhill or Ardnacrusha power house, but would never get past them. The fish passes were entirely inadequate to their needs, presenting them with a series of obstacles that only the strongest of them could ever hope to conquer. A major issue that remained was the fact that because most of the water was being used by the Ardnacrusha power station to generate electricity, not enough was left flowing over the passes for them to operate efficiently. This had been going on for years.

From 1984, I was involved in the Irish Estuaries Salmon Net-Fishermen's Association, which represented hereditary net fishermen from the four provinces of Ireland. Our stated objectives were to represent fishermen licensed to fish for salmon, and to get the government to formulate a policy of conservation and management free from political interference. We aimed to enable ordinary people to make a living fishing salmon in a sustainable way, as their ancestors had for generations.

I travelled the length and breadth of the country, talking to net-fishermen from estuarine areas similar to mine. It was the same story everywhere. Their livelihoods had been compromised by hydroelectricity for decades. They were under attack on the one side by high and escalating levels of pollution and on the other by rampant salmon-poaching at sea. Of every hundred salmon that should have returned to their natal rivers to spawn, typically only about three did. In practically every salmon river in the country, the numbers of wild salmon were so low it was plain that the species was nearing extinction.

I also visited seaports all over Ireland's coast, where I met the smaller fishermen working the coastal areas, and saw the huge trawlers further out to sea. We smaller operators all felt that the minister responsible for the fisheries at the time, Paddy O'Toole, urgently needed to do better at enforcing the salmon conservation laws. He had to crack down on the illegal fisheries that were devastating Ireland's salmon population.

A further blow was that the traditional relationship between fishermen and fishmongers had been damaged beyond recognition. When I was a child, the fishermen and the fishmongers had enjoyed a mutually beneficial, respectful and collegial relationship. We had provided the fishmongers with fish, and they had given us a fair price for it. Many fishmongers also provided credit, at a fairly reasonable rate, to fishermen who needed to get new gear at the beginning of the season. Now, when fishermen arrived with their modest catches from the River Shannon, the prices they were offered were risibly low. When they protested that they could not survive on what they were being paid, the fishmongers just shrugged – they could get salmon from fish farms for a fraction of what the fishermen were asking for, and even if some customers prized the wild fish, others could not even tell the difference, or preferred an inferior product at a lower price.

By the mid-1980s, optimism about the government's plans to restock the Shannon and other freshwater courses with artificially bred salmon was seriously on the wane. The numbers of salmon in the river, which had been briefly inflated by the hatchery programme, had given rise to false hope, which was dashed as the wild salmon population fell even further. Almost half of the artificially bred fish died within two or three days of being released into the ecosystem, while most of the rest failed to breed, failed to thrive or were consumed by predators in greater numbers than normal. Having been raised in cages, their survival instincts had never developed. Often they could not even identify the species that predated on them and practically swam into the open jaws of a waiting carnivore, as though they had a death-wish. They often did not even seem able to manage normal shifts and changes in the environment. Even an unusually high tide could result in thousands of hatchery fish – many of them immediately recognisable by their removed adipose fins – simply getting washed up onto the riverbanks to die.

In 1985, those of us who still fished the Shannon Estuary cooperated with the formation of a nature sanctuary there, and from that period on, nobody used drift nets in that area. Within a few years, we were seeing dolphins where they had not been seen for years – proof that such straight-forward measures can lead to positive results quite quickly. In general, however, the depredation of Irish waters persisted.

Even though issues of overfishing and corruption in the fisheries was quite well covered in the media, the public appetite for salmon remained higher than ever. Cynical politicians pushed for more and more boats, with bigger and bigger nets, to fish at sea. Fishermen started eyeing up waters far away from those they were legally allowed to fish in.

What happened in one part of the North Atlantic region affected all of it. Greenland officially left the EEC in 1985, following its referendum in 1982. The campaign to leave had focused mostly on disputes over fishing rights.

This was catastrophic news for the salmon that travelled to Greenland waters to feed, and for the Irish and other European fishermen who depended on them, because now European legislation did not apply to them. Drastic overfishing in the waters of Greenland was the inevitable consequence.

Most of the people in Greenland are indigenous Inuit, a people that has been treated appallingly for generations. Traditionally, the Inuit survived the harsh, challenging climate by hunting and fishing, and because their own numbers were always quite low, the amount they needed to take to survive was relatively little. Now the native Greenlanders could be cynically exploited by other governments and used as a front for severe overfishing of their rich waters.

By 1987, governments in Ireland and elsewhere in the EEC were discussing the possibility of offering compensation to fishermen in order to reduce the drift netting of salmon.[113] At this stage, the Minister of State at the Department of the Marine was Pat 'the Cope' Gallagher, from Burtonport in Donegal. Pat's well-known interests in the salmon industry had made him wealthy long before he entered politics. His vested interests suggested to me that he might have a compromised ability to be objective when it came to administering the marine sector, and I had little faith that he would do so in a reasonable way.

Pat hobnobbed with sea fishermen all over Ireland, promising them the world. He criticised foreign trawlers for the overfishing they were doing off Irish coasts, while ignoring the fact that Irish trawlers were doing exactly the same thing, even when they were caught exceeding quotas in international waters.[114] He supported the interests of salmon farms,[115] even as evidence emerged of the damage that these were doing to the environment.

While the fishermen and salmon farmers of Donegal and others coastal waters may have been pleased with his work on their behalf, those of us who fished the rivers – and all those concerned about the environment in general – were less than impressed. The Central Fisheries Board – the coordinating agency for the seven regional fisheries boards – called for a complete end to offshore salmon fishing, and recommended the fishing of ranched fish in inland locations as an alternative.[116] There was a lot of talk about the government paying compensation to those whose livelihoods had been destroyed by the decline in traditional fishing. Some people held out great hopes that they would get a big handout, with which they might be able to start a new business. Some got rich, while small-scale fishermen fled the industry. Intimidation and even violence now became part of life, as growing numbers of trawler owners made good livings from compensation schemes that seemed to overlook those who needed help the most.

Meanwhile, the North Western Fishery Board continued to call for seal culls, claiming hyperbolically that 'human food is destroyed in a world of 4000 million [seal] mouths',[117] at a time when 80 per cent of the salmon captured by humans was now taken at sea by way of indiscriminate trawler fishing.[118] The reality was that, in areas like Donegal, over 50 per cent of the local salmon catch was taken – by well-equipped human beings, not hungry seals – illegally, outside the twelve mile limit.[119]

National and regional newspapers published lengthy articles on the question of mooted drift-net bans for the sea fisheries, but arguments in favour of a ban focused on Ireland's potential to develop a lucrative tourist business based around angling for salmon.[120] Few journalists covering the topic even mentioned the situation facing families like mine, which had been making their living from small-scale inland fishing for generations.

All the rivers in Ireland, like the Irish environment in general, were facing significant challenges from ongoing and escalating pollution relating to industry, agriculture and sewerage. Towns and cities continued to discharge untreated, raw sewage. By 1988, a county councillor in the Shannon region angrily remarked that a 'condom licence' would be more useful than a fishing license, as the river was 'full' of condoms, which frequently washed up on the riverbanks,[121] both a revolting spectacle and a hazard to wildlife.

Fish farms, which had been making good money for their owners since the early 1970s, continued to open. They required a licence, and Minister Paddy O'Toole had stated that fish farms would only proceed where they would not conflict with 'other fishing, tourist, navigational, and environmental interests',[122] but it seemed clear that they were effectively being green-lit despite the increasingly well-understood environmental hazards associated with them. The Irish government provided them with enormous subsidies and overlooked both the colossal mortality rates of salmon in captivity and the incredible damage that they were causing to the environment.

The quality of life experienced by the fish in fish farms was extremely poor. Many of them were essentially rotting, even as they clung to life for just long enough to be turned into low-quality food products. The exact same picture could be seen in every Atlantic region where salmon were farmed.

The ESB already had a large weir across the river at Limerick City – the Thomond Weir – and thus an effective monopoly over the fish on the Shannon. They also had a huge financial incentive to get into farming, especially because the government was giving very generous subsidies to fish farms – up to 80 per cent of the cost of establishing a farm. Salmon farming remained a growth industry.

While most fishing communities had been broadly welcoming of fish farming when it started out, now they were increasingly cynical. Did salmon farming really relieve pressure on the wild population, as fish farmers claimed, or did it actually just cause a whole new set of problems? Either way, the ESB was now getting in on the game.

The ESB had previously accepted – at least on paper – that it had a duty of care to the wild fish that lived in the waters now harnessed for hydroelectricity. This included the Shannon, the Lee and the Erne. It was thus difficult to understand why the ESB was now getting into commercial fish farming. This was surely not part of its remit.

In 1987, Salmara, a subsidiary entity owned by the ESB, was incorporated and started operating salmon farms. That year, it made profits of £800,000 on a turnover of £3,000,000, in what *The Irish Times* described as the 'rapidly expanding' fish farming sector.[123] By 1988, Salmara worked with local interests to open new farms in Inver, County Donegal, and Castletownbere, County Cork. Salmara had the full support of the Department of the Marine, and employed 110 full-time staff.[124] Between 1982 and 1989, the number of salmon produced in Irish fish farms grew rapidly, from 100 to 7000 tonnes.[125] Ireland was now hailed as a world leader in the growth industry of fish farming.[126]

In 1989, the ESB – rather astonishingly, given that Salmara was raising fish for human consumption – stated that it had no responsibility to report on pollution caused by agricultural, domestic and industrial effluent entering the rivers and lakes under its control, while adding that it had carried out works to improve the fishing and spawning grounds of the Shannon.[127]

Inevitably, some of the farmed salmon escaped into the rivers, bringing their high rates of parasitic infestation and disease with them, which then spread to an already seriously struggling wild population. Still, the proponents of fish farming – including the government agencies that were subsidising and supporting them – continued to promote it as an environmentally friendly, sustainable way of meeting the public's demand for fish. That it appeared so at a glance is entirely understandable. The idea of eating fish that have been raised in captivity, and therefore letting the wild ones live with minimal disruption, is a simple, attractive one.

The reality, however, was that the fish farms that were beginning to proliferate were not nearly as sustainable as their promotors suggested. The farmed fish needed to eat, and as most of them ate other marine species, wild fish were used to create fishmeal to feed them with. So vast quantities of fish were still being removed from the wild, but now, instead of being used to feed people, they were used to feed other fish, which in turn compromised the wild fish by introducing disease and parasites. Salmon farming was clearly an environmental disaster on all fronts.

In 1988, now in early middle age, I returned to London for work, this time as a hire agency lorry driver. Most of my earnings went towards additional flying lessons at Red Hill Aerodrome in Surrey. I stayed in London for about a year, making good money and, once again, I toyed with the idea of staying and putting down roots in England. But the money and opportunities were not enough to make me want to stay away forever, and I came back home again. Although I did not know it at the time, that would be my last extended stay in London. I have many fond memories of my times there over the years. The city and its people still have a special place in my heart, and always will.

Back in Ireland, I was still living in the house where I had spent my teenage years. Coonagh had changed immeasurably from when I was growing up. So many people from my generation had already left. My siblings had married, moved out – emigrated, in some cases – and started families of their own. Mam was getting older, and of course she missed Dad, but she was strong and tough and still had a very active social life. Having always been a broad-minded, inquisitive woman, she was taking in her stride the extraordinary social changes that had been going on for decades, and that seemed to be accelerating now. Some of those changes, like improvements in the standards of education and of housing, were very welcome. Others, like the growing disconnect between the local people and the physical environment in which they lived, were not. They were disturbing and somewhat baffling to someone like her, who had spent so much of her life following the cycles of the seasons and their influence on farming, fishing and the natural world.

* * *

On 9 March 1990, Paddy Moriarty – who had been the Chief Executive of the ESB since 1981 – addressed the controversies associated with salmon fishing in a speech given to the Tralee Chamber of Commerce. Paddy, a proud Kerryman, stated that the ESB had no intention of making money at the expense of the environment. It had gone into salmon farming out of a sense of patriotic duty, to 'create jobs' and 'share wealth', and thus to help halt the depopulation of rural Ireland.

Those words rang very hollow to anyone involved in the fisheries. It was estimated that in the previous seven years, from 1983 to 1990, numbers of wild salmon had declined precipitously, from about seven million to five million.[128]

Overfishing at sea remained a huge and growing problem, with ever-bigger boats taking all they could get, vastly exceeding the quotas they had been given, and the government authorities largely failing to apprehend the worst offenders.

In 1990, a terrible tragedy occurred in the waters off Ballycotton in east Cork. Four experienced fishery officers – Barry O'Driscoll, Barra Ó Longaigh, Dominic Meehan and Benno Haussmann – set off from Ringaskiddy in poor weather conditions at seven in the morning on 7 July in a fifteen-foot launch, the *Setanta*. Also on board was Michael Fanning from Fermoy. They were on patrol, monitoring the waters for illegal fishing. They found an illegal monofilament drift net and pulled it onboard, but tragedy struck when their boat capsized. The men went overboard and the four fishery officers drowned.[129]

As the dust settled, all sorts of rumours swirled about the exact nature of the accident, and whether the fisheries officers could have been saved if the will had been there for it. The sole survivor, Michael, described a fishing boat going past them. At that time, all the men in the water were still alive, calling out and blowing in unison on their international-standard, high-decibel emergency whistles for help.[130] The people on the boat did not hear them, such was the weather.

Of the five brave fishery officers in this case, four had now lost their lives in carrying out their duties. There was so much money in illegal fishing then, and so much bad blood across the fishing industry in general, that nobody seemed to trust anyone and there appeared to be no way forward.

* * *

As my everyday life of fishing and activism grew progressively more stressful, I needed an escape valve. Always on the search for a new challenge, I trained as a parachutist at the Clonbullogue airfield, north of Portarlington. I saw this as a natural extension of having learned how to fly, and having qualified as a pilot for parachutists. The first thing you feel when you jump is fear, which is rapidly replaced by exhilaration, and finally settles on a profound sense of peace. To this day, I tell everyone who asks about it that learning how to jump from a small plane taught me almost as much about flying as learning to be a pilot. From then on, both parachuting and flying helped me to put my worries into perspective.

One of my biggest aerial adventures took place in 1990, when Ireland was in the World Cup in Italy. As a paid-up member of the club, I had the use of a four-seater international touring aircraft. Together with my nephew Pat, who had jacked in a job on a building site in London for the purpose, I flew all the way to Rome. We eyed the boats at work on the blue Mediterranean far below us, and stopped off at the various match venues, including Sardinia and Sicily, on the way. We stayed for a month. It was the experience of a lifetime. Not for the first time, I congratulated myself on having exchanged the life of a drinker for that of a pilot.

After the trip, I returned to the reality of salmon fishing, and an increasingly grim situation.

Looking back now, this was the moment when I definitively severed all ties with London. I didn't make a conscious decision to stop going to London periodically for work, but now I was so busy with the Fishery Board that even if I had wanted to go, I would not have had the time. I started to attend all the meetings and talks, and tried to learn as much as I could about the governance of fishing; for this I received from the Board my expenses and a daily stipend.

I was unconvinced that the Board was really as impartial as it was supposed to be. While it did seem to represent the interests of well-connected, wealthy trawler owners, it seemed to have little interest in the welfare of traditional small-scale fishermen, and even less in the welfare of the fish. In many ways, this was a dark and depressing period in my life. The stark reality of what was happening to the salmon, and of the devastation being wreaked on the Shannon in general, was hitting me hard. I found some solace in starting to fight back, and a lot in taking to the air whenever the opportunity arose.

As my aircraft left the ground and took to the sky, the landscape that I knew as well as I knew my own face was gloriously laid out below me. Far beneath the plane, I could see the form of the River Shannon snaking through the countryside, the many rivulets and streams that fed it, and the different shades of green in the fields that surrounded it. I soared over ancient ring forts and what remained of the homes of the generations of fishing people who had gone before.

Growing up in Coonagh, I had always been very aware of the past. It was all around us, in the form of castles, old houses and forts. Famine-era potato drills and half-grown-over old graveyards dotted the landscape. It was there, too, in the stories that the older people related at get-togethers in people's homes. From the sky now, I could see how Ireland's past was literally etched onto the landscape, creating a map of time and human endeavour as well as of geography.

The influence of the Ardnacrusha electrical plant on the behaviour of the water was clearly visible from above. So were the sewer and waste-water outlets of towns and cities, spewing their loads into the river. I could track the urban sprawl of Limerick City, already impacting dramatically on the way of life of my native Coonagh.

Much as my flying brought me joy, it also added to my concern that a tipping point had been reached in terms of the health of the Shannon and of the wider environment. Far below, I could see tiny gandelows at work, fewer of them with each year that passed. When I looked at the coastal regions, I observed hundreds of large craft illicitly fishing the coastal waters for the few salmon that had made it that far, and that would now not reach their natal rivers.

This situation simply could not continue indefinitely. The end of the Atlantic wild salmon was in sight. The River Shannon and the land it travelled through were despoiled, ever emptier of native wildlife. The sights and sounds of nature that had once filled the area were missing, unseen and unheard by the younger generations.

Mam, who had lived through and seen so much, was getting on in years now. As we lived together, and I drove her everywhere she needed to go, we had become very close. I was very proud of her when, in her mid-eighties, she took a flight for the first time. She was thrilled with herself after her trip to New York to see my brother Tony, with plenty to say about all that she had seen.

Mam's mind was as sharp as ever as she also continued to relate the old stories about what the area had been like when she was young. Although many of her stories were familiar to me, I never got tired of listening to them. It was astonishing to think about all the things that she had seen, and how very dramatically the area had changed.

CHAPTER EIGHT

Technology Versus Nature

Fishermen from communities like Coonagh now despaired of ever seeing an improvement in the estuarine and river environment they lived and worked in. The natural environment in general, and the salmon population in particular, were under sustained attack from all fronts. It looked increasingly like an unstoppable disaster. The impacts on life in Coonagh were far-reaching. Every fisherman in Coonagh had, at some stage, been in a crew with every other fisherman. Inevitably, all those hours on the water had brought the men very close together. When we were children, our dirty faces were almost as likely to be wiped clean by someone else's mother as by our own. And because our fathers worked together, our families had passed through times of plenty and times of financial difficulty together.

I do not want to romanticise life in rural Limerick prior to the industrialisation of the area, because it was often very difficult. But the old closeness, the strong sense of community, had been marvellous. Now that the local fishery had collapsed, fathers – and increasingly mothers too – were mostly working in factories. Life was a lot easier in many ways, and all of the children were getting a good education, but they no longer drifted in and out of each other's homes like they used to. And even though most adults did not have to work nearly as hard as the older generation had, they also seemed to have much less time to spend together.

My own family was quite typical: several of my siblings were delighted with their new jobs in industry. They continued to take an interest in the Shannon fishery, and always asked how a particular season was going, but they loved the fact that they could provide well and reliably for their kids. They also enjoyed having their evenings to themselves, instead of trying to get a few hours' sleep before heading out for a shift fishing on the river.

My sisters and their women friends were mostly delighted with the new status quo. They knew well how hard it had been for their mothers to make ends meet with income from the fisheries and irregular, tough work like farm labouring, which their mothers and fathers had done seasonally. Now women flocked into the factories for work. They could stop for a while to mind their kids if they wanted to, and then pick it up again afterwards. Most of them seemed to love the freedom they gained from earning a good salary on their own.

'You'd want to be getting sense at your age,' I often heard from well-meaning relatives, now that I was in my forties. 'It's not too late to get a good job at the factory. It's no life for you, trying to make a living on that aul' river. And what about a pension?'

I could see the benefits of the new way of life, but I wasn't alone in desperately missing the camaraderie of the old ways, and mourning for a time when the Shannon had been filled with boats and the sound of men at work on them. The other remaining fishermen and I did our utmost to keep the best of the old ways alive.

Looking back now, I think one of the biggest losses to the local men in particular was losing the chance to talk. Irish men have the deserved reputation of not talking about themselves and their feelings very much, but as a fishing shift can last for hours, with two, three or four men who had known one another since childhood working closely together, those were times when they did confide in each other. Now that they worked on assembly lines or drove forklifts, that opportunity for open conversation had gone away.

The older people who had grown up fishing and were now gradually populating the graveyards were laid to rest beneath expensive, highly polished gravestones. In earlier times, most local families had not been able to afford anything of the sort. Gravestones were simple, or were absent, with a just flimsy temporary marker in place instead. Sometimes there was nothing at all to show that someone who had once been deeply loved was now beneath the soil. Now, in recognition of their fathers' and grandfathers' work as fishermen, some of these families arranged for stonemasons to decorate swanky gravestones with gilded engravings of the leaping salmon that had been their lifelong obsession. The irony was that there were very few of those salmon left.

✳ ✳ ✳

In about 1990, I was introduced to an Icelander, Orri Vigfússon, who had recently established the North Atlantic Salmon Fund, a fund to help save the Atlantic wild salmon. He wanted to meet someone from the Limerick area who could describe their experience of the fisheries here. Orri had grown up in a herring-fishing community in northern Iceland.

While they are much smaller, herring are not too dissimilar from the salmon, and can be caught using similar techniques. When Orri was a kid, the people of his community had been forced to hang up their nets and put away their boats, as overfishing of herring had destroyed their business. As an adult, Orri was a very successful businessman, but he still felt a huge sense of attachment to the traditional ways of life and to the well-being of natural watercourses and the species that live in them. He was also an intrepid angler, who loved taking his rods and going fishing at weekends.

Like many others around the North Atlantic region, Orri could see that the salmon was rapidly approaching extinction, largely because of a combination of overfishing and the infrastructure associated with hydroelectricity. His fund proposed that most coastal fishing operations of salmon, particularly drift netting, should be stopped throughout the North Atlantic. Buyouts of nets and compensation to affected fishermen would be offered, so that they could retrain and move into other areas of work. This would protect salmon in the ocean, leaving many more of them to return to their natal rivers, relieving pressure on the species, while also preserving the wild population so that small-scale local fisheries – mostly inland fisheries – and angling could survive. Orri further proposed that groups of ordinary people approach their governments and influential members of the fishing industry with a plan to save both the salmon and the small-scale traditional fisheries. He had already made some connections among local Irish anglers, and was now anxious to learn more about river fishing in Irish salmon waters more generally. When I heard that Orri was coming to Limerick, I was eager to meet up with him, as his ideas were very interesting.

I invited Orri to accompany me on a flight over the Shannon, to see the river and estuary from above, as well as the many boats out at sea. We met at the airfield in Coonagh, and after speaking with him for just a little while, I was very impressed by Orri's deep knowledge of the salmon, by his down-to-earth attitude and by the fact that he had invested a huge amount of his own money to get the fund started. This was someone who did not just talk, as so many did, but who acted. Orri was upbeat as he climbed into the little two-seater plane, excited about the trip and the prospect of seeing the Shannon estuary and the Atlantic coast from the air.

It was a wonderful day for flying a light aircraft – not too windy and with excellent visibility. I had taken to the air from Coonagh more times than I could count, but it had never stopped being thrilling, and it was a pleasure to be able to take someone like Orri with me. Once we were up and had levelled off, we followed the Shannon down from Coonagh to the mouth of the estuary. There, and further out to sea, we could see the fishing boats at work. Orri was extremely knowledgeable – he could identify at a glance the diverse types of boat, and knew what each was capable of. Orri commented straight away that the number of boats fishing for salmon was incompatible with the species' survival in the Shannon. The numbers just did not add up. You cannot take and take and take and expect nature to keep on giving.

After our flight, over cups of tea at the clubhouse, Orri said he was extremely pessimistic about the future of the Atlantic wild salmon. What he had seen suggested a population in precipitous decline, heading rapidly towards extinction. This was consistent with what I had learned too, even though some fishermen still insisted that they were getting good catches and the numbers were still high.

Orri left me with a lot to think about. He came from a family with a long history in fishing, much like mine, and knew just as I did how difficult it would be to impose bans and restrictions without providing alternative means for people to make a living. While Orri himself was wealthy, he had grown up in an ordinary fishing community and he understood the struggles of working people who depend on a wild species for their livelihood. At the time, Orri's view that drift netting should be banned completely struck me as excessive, although I also recognised that he was a person to be taken seriously.

As someone who still made his living from fishing, I could see both sides. Although I was increasingly alarmed about the situation for the salmon, I also knew that a complete ban on drift nets would be devastating for many families, and would impact seriously on coastal communities that depended on fishing to survive.

In those days, I thought of myself as a pragmatic conservationist. I recognised that radical steps were required to save the salmon, and I hoped that action could be taken in a way that also conserved the fisheries, including drift netting in moderation. Looking back now, I can see that I was still quite naïve. Even though I knew that the salmon were in a dire situation, I was hopeful that the will was there to remedy it, and that there were enough salmon to bounce back if they were given a fighting chance.

After that first meeting, Orri and I remained in contact. We spoke on the phone often, exchanged emails and met up whenever the opportunity arose. Gradually I came to accept that Orri was right: nothing less than a complete ban on drift netting would do. Together, we would meet many government ministers and officials, who generally started off saying all the right things, but quickly demonstrated that they did not have a clue.

Because of the circles he moved in, Orri was able to secure meetings with diplomats and ambassadors from all across the Atlantic region, including senior staff at the American embassy, in the hope that he could persuade them to work together to save the salmon. Everyone made polite noises, but ultimately effected little to no change.

In 1991, the year of Paddy Moriarty's departure from the ESB, it reported the worst year for salmon on the Shannon since 1984.[131] Salmon farming may have been contributing some jobs in the Atlantic coastal region, but it was destroying livelihoods on the Shannon. The inland fisheries were also losing out because of the rampant illegal overfishing in the Atlantic, and appalling levels of pollution. After decades of fishing, I was keenly aware of the fishermen's need for representation, so in 1992, I put myself forward for the Fisheries Board, and was elected to represent the licensed drift-net fishermen of the Shannon Estuary.

Meanwhile, around the world, alarm bells were ringing about the state of the oceans and seas, and bodies with responsibility for them started to at least talk about taking action. In May 1992, the Food and Agricultural Organisation of the United Nations – the FAO – held an International Conference on Responsible Fishing in Cancún, Mexico. Delegates discussed how to balance the need to preserve the marine environment – in the context of rapidly expanding fisheries, particularly on the high seas – with protecting communities that depended on fish to eat.

That the meeting took place at all was a major step. I remember reading about it at the time and feeling pleased that something was happening at the highest levels, but also feeling sceptical that it would make any difference. I doubted that most fishermen the world over were even aware that the meeting had taken place; certainly, very few in Ireland knew.

And even if they had, it probably would have seemed utterly irrelevant – years of experience had shown that government bodies and international organisations said all sorts of things and signed all sorts of agreements, but actually did very little.

On the ground, nothing changed, because nothing ever did. Overfishing continued in Irish waters and everywhere else, too. Hydroelectric plants still blocked the passage of the dwindling populations of migrating fish and caused massive environmental problems, even as hydroelectricity continued to be hailed as a cleaner way of generating power. Pollution of all sorts continued to seep and pour into bodies of water of every kind. Innovative technologies continued to come onto the market, improving the efficiency of how fish were captured. Fishermen had been using sturdy nylon nets since the 1960s, if not before, and these were getting better and better. Increasingly, they were now using monofilament nets of materials that were less destructible than ever. The new generations of monofilament nets were all but invisible to fish and other marine species, and when they got lost at sea, or were deliberately discarded, they became so-called 'ghost nets' that moved through the water on their own, gathering and destroying sea life as they travelled. Many nets were discarded by trawlers, so much so that it was practically routine. By this time, the estuarine areas of salmon rivers, and tidal rivers like the Shannon, the Barrow and the Lee, were significantly depleted.

In my childhood, the fisherman had still thought of himself as engaged in a sort of battle of wits with the fish he caught. His traditional knowledge of the tides and the movement of the fish guided him to the fishing grounds, where his hemp net and small boat could take in a modest catch. Now a well-equipped boat and crew, with the latest sonar and radio equipment, could take in enormous numbers of fish, wiping out in a matter of just a few years the remaining population's natural capacity to reproduce. The smaller fishermen found it increasingly difficult to catch anything, while large, well-equipped boats hoovered up the few fish that had evaded capture in the feeding grounds of Greenland or the Faroes and the coastal areas of Ireland, and were now trying to get home to spawn. The entire salmon fishing industry thus became dependent on ranched fish that had started life in hatcheries.

Meanwhile, the general public – increasingly urban, increasingly wealthy and increasingly divorced from the often ugly realities of food production – had grown accustomed to the constant availability of inexpensive meat and fish. The fish was always in stock in the local supermarket, already cut and wrapped, bearing little resemblance to the living creatures that had supplied them. Most consumers had no idea how destructive fish farming was proving to be to the natural environment, and if they did read anything about it, they did not care.

As fishing in open waters became ever more damaging to the wild environment, the number of fish farms in cages at sea, in locations such as Bantry Bay and waters off Donegal, Galway and Mayo, also continued to grow, and alongside it the growth in escapees and disease among the wild populations.

Over the course of the 1970s and '80s, the relationship between traditional fishmongers and fishermen had been badly damaged as a result of the growth in fish farming. Now, in the 1990s, the traditional fishmonger businesses that had long brokered the relationship between fishing people and consumers were disappearing rapidly too. They were being squeezed out of business by the huge supermarkets that occupied vast tracts of land on the outskirts of towns and cities. Fishermen and fishmongers who had once earned a decent living were struggling even to pay for the basic necessities of life, while consumers were buying flabby, unhealthy farmed fish, and allegedly 'wild' ranched fish, under the misinformed belief that the industry that ensured refrigerator cabinets were constantly stocked with precut salmon darnes was actually providing them with a healthy product to feed their families.

But many of these fish were living with – and dying with, if not dying of – viral and fungal infections, bacterial diseases such as furunculosis, out-of-control infestations of parasites and chronic stress. While perhaps the research on what eating diseased salmon does to humans was still inadequate, simple common sense suggests that it is probably not very good for us.

I had always been as comfortable immersed in nature as in my own home. As I became increasingly alarmed by what I was seeing every time I went out in my little gandelow – which itself was happening less and less often as the fishing season, which had once lasted for months, was now down to a few weeks – I realised that I needed to learn a lot more. I needed to know what was happening elsewhere, and I needed to augment my considerable traditionally acquired knowledge of the salmon and its environment with an academic understanding.

Through my activism, the various groups I was involved in and the many interesting people I was meeting as a result, I gained access to all the latest research in the form of lectures, notes and reading material. I started to read all the academic and scientific literature about fish, river ecosystems and the environment that I could get my hands on, thankful that I had been born into the first generation in my family to get a good secondary education and that I could understand the academic language such articles were written in. One by one, the truths that I and other local fishermen already knew from experience started to fit together like a jigsaw puzzle, gradually revealing a picture of environmental mismanagement that was devastating, and that went far beyond the island of Ireland.

At this time, I still depended on the Shannon for my livelihood. As the number of salmon had dropped so low, my main source of income then came from cutting the reeds growing along the riverbanks, binding them into sheaves and selling them into the thatching industry. Fortunately, at that time the government was providing funding and subsidies to the owners of thatched homes and to thatchers, having recognised that these houses were a vital element of Irish material culture. There was a mini-boom of thatching on the go as growing numbers of young people were training as thatchers and putting new roofs on traditional homes around the country. This was a blessing to me, because if I had been relying solely on what I could make from salmon-fishing, it would have been impossible for me to stay in Coonagh, and I did not want to go anywhere else.

But even cutting the reeds was not like it used to be. When I was growing up, you would generally see other reed-cutters hard at work when you went out to do it, and there were typically two or three men on each of the gandelows. Now I was usually all alone on a silent river, and while reed-cutting takes place near the shore and is less dangerous than fishing, it is never really a good idea to go out by yourself – you can get a rope tangled around your ankle, get pulled overboard and be taken by the river.

The Irish Seal Sanctuary was founded in Skerries, County Dublin, by a biologist called Brendan Price, who was very familiar with the seal population in that area and alarmed by the calls for a seal cull that were frequently aired in the media. I think the first time I met Brendan was at a lecture about the environment in Trinity College, Dublin. Brendan and his colleagues, who included a fisheries officer called Johnny Woodlock, had come together to raise awareness of the potential of seals as part of a tourist industry, to rehabilitate and release injured wild seals, and to highlight the fact that a seal cull would not address the problems of overfishing. Thereafter we met often at these meetings, and periodically spoke on the phone.

Brendan was very interested to hear about what was happening at sea with fishermen's drift nets, as they were impacting directly on the seals. I was fascinated by the depths of his knowledge. We both agreed that calls for a seal cull were a nonsense, a transparent attempt to blame seals for an environmental catastrophe that was entirely the fault of human beings.

My relationship with the Seal Sanctuary was formalised in 1993 when I joined its Fishers' Advisory Group. This consisted of various people who worked in fishing and also understood the importance of the wider environment, and the need for fishing people to work in harmony with the environment as a whole. I was delighted to be on board. It may sound strange to anyone not in the fishing industry, but it took courage for those of us advising the Seal Sanctuary to do so in a public way. We were often vilified and even threatened by other fishermen, who either believed the story that seals were to blame for the declining numbers of fish, or wanted to propagate this idea because it removed the focus from the topic of overfishing at sea. More than once, I was advised that terrible accidents can happen on a boat, and that I would want to watch myself in case something terrible happened to me. It was impossible to know how serious or otherwise the threats were, but also impossible to dismiss them as just talk.

Everyone involved in the Seal Sanctuary came from a different background, and we were all brought together by a common interest in ecology and animal welfare. The sanctuary frequently collected injured seals, many of which had been found with pieces of indestructible nylon net wound around their bodies. On various occasions, I found myself transporting a seal in the back of my van – wrapped in wet clothes to keep it cool and wet. They would be going to the Sanctuary for treatment, or back to the sea to be returned to the wild. It would bring to mind the old stories Mam and Dad had sometimes related, about enchanted seals that could take on the shape of human beings when they came to land. Perhaps those old stories had something to say, in a symbolic way, about the fact that humans and animals alike are all part of the natural world.

* * *

Like most people, when salmon farming had started in a big way in Ireland in the 1970s, I had no idea what a challenge it was going to pose to the wild salmon and to the natural environment in general. By now, I had a very good understanding of it, because I could see for myself the damage the fish farms were doing. In 1993, the ESB published an annual report that stated, among other things, that its subsidiary organisation, Salmara Fisheries, was now Ireland's largest producer of caged farmed salmon, with 160 full-time staff. This was presented as an entirely positive thing – they were creating jobs and opportunities in remote parts of the country where work prospects were otherwise limited. The report referred testily to criticism of fish farming, stated that Salmara 'co-operates fully with the Department of the Marine and Fishery Boards' and complained that critics were having a negative impact on the creation of sustainable employment. It made no mention of the real environmental challenges posed by salmon farming, or of the wild salmon and the ESB's duty of care to them.[132] At that time, Ireland was still emerging from the terrible economic crisis of the 1980s, and people were understandably very anxious about the future; the ESB was reflecting the national mood.

Then, in 1994, the ESB sought approval from the government to sell its four offshore salmon farms. That permission was granted in January 1995. The sale of these farms, as well as a smolt-rearing operation at Lough Allen, a lake on the Shannon in County Leitrim, realised £4.5 million.[133] The ESB never really explained why it had gone into salmon farming in the first place, or why – after just a few years, having apparently been successful in financial terms – it got out of it. Given the negative publicity that was increasingly being aired about salmon fishing and the many harms it causes to the environment, it is tempting to assume that the ESB was concerned that the optics just were not very good.

While fish farmers and investors in fish farming were brushing aside environmental and other concerns about the industry, other sectors appeared to be in denial about the reality facing the remaining Atlantic salmon. In 1996, the report of the Task Force on Salmon Management, chaired by Professor Noel Wilkins of the National University of Ireland (NUI) Galway, was published. It recommended a scheme involving tagging salmon to trace where they were being caught and sold, and introducing quotas to manage the numbers caught, as well as reducing the length of the commercial season, and restricting the inshore fishing limits to six miles. None of this went nearly far enough to avoid the looming environmental disaster. The report, controversially, also recommended legalising the use of monofilament drift nets for salmon, on the grounds that fishermen were using them anyway.[134]

The new tags used to identify hatchery salmon were presented as being tamper-proof. The heavy-duty plastic loops were printed with data that identified where the salmon came from, and fishermen could cooperate by providing vital data and contributing to the administration of quotas. Fishermen quickly discovered that it was actually quite easy to open a 'tamper-proof' tag – if boiled until the rigid plastic softened, it could be opened and could be used repeatedly. Fishermen were supposed to keep extensive log books, detailing how many salmon they had caught and where, and what they did with them. Many of them registered a relatively small number of sales to fishmongers and private customers, while maintaining that the bulk of the catch was for private use. Of course, the reality was that massive quantities of salmon were being sold on the black market. Everyone, from the Fishery Board down to the smallest fisherman, knew that the tagging system was essentially a State-sponsored scam.

By now, Ardnacrusha power station was beginning to show its age. Ireland had been fully electrified for decades, and hydroelectricity was now providing a small proportion of the power needed to run the country. Ardnacrusha had been a mainstay of Ireland's plan to modernise back in the 1920s and '30s, but now there were many other power stations, and it was delivering a much smaller percentage of the country's electricity needs.

At this stage, the government could have taken the bold step of decommissioning Ardnacrusha, replacing it with a less damaging way of generating power, and could have altered the infrastructure to accommodate other uses. This would have given the River Shannon a chance to restore itself, and made Ireland a world leader in environmental policy. Building the Ardnacrusha station and nationalising electricity in the 1920s had been a bold step, which had impressed the world at the time. Destroying the hydroelectrical plant seventy years later and letting the river heal itself would have been another bold move. Of course, it did not happen.

Instead, the government decided to refurbish the station, making it possible to control it remotely.[135] Previously, it had been operated by a tiny permanent workforce, augmented by a seasonal cadre of local labourers. Once the initial construction had been completed, the ESB actually employed very few local people and had a rather poor reputation with respect to how they were treated. In 1996, a new control room was added at the end of the turbine hall, with a computer-aided management-information system and control functions. New transformers were installed, and three of the old turbines were replaced with more modern models.

I believe that the renovations made matters even worse for the Shannon, and particularly for its ecology. Before, at least the people running Ardnacrusha had been located in the area, with an understanding of the local environment and a sense of investment in the community. Now decisions were made at a central location, far away.

I was in my mid-fifties then, living out my middle years torn between anger and hope – anger because I could see what was happening to the salmon and how the authorities were not doing nearly enough to save it; and hope that if only the general public could be made to understand the gravity of the situation, something would change.

Fishing was still my primary source of income. Although hardly anyone else was doing it full-time on the river, I could usually cobble together a crew by reaching out to local men who used holiday time to do some fishing, who would do a few hours of a night shift on the river after work, or put in a day or two at the weekend. As the composition of these little crews changed so often, our conversation was never quite as in-depth as in the old days, when you might share your gandelow with the same couple of lads for weeks or even months at a time.

At this point, the dramatic cultural and economic changes that had started taking shape even before I was born were manifesting in the lives of my now-adult nieces and nephews. Many of them had settled in the area – they had been able to at least in part because there were so many good jobs locally, far more than there had been before. But they had lost the deep connection to the Shannon area that had been part of our family life for generations. I was happy to see them all doing so well, and enjoying a standard of living that my own parents would have found almost impossible to imagine, but I was sorry that they and their children would never know what it was like to see the River Shannon full of life. My own childhood beside and on the river had been such a source of fun and excitement to me, it was difficult to imagine what it must be like growing up near the Shannon but not knowing it the way I did. Then again, thirty years before, working in London, I had been aghast to see the filth of the Thames and to realise that it was a dead river, incapable of supporting life. The Shannon – which had been compromised anyway since the construction of the power plant – was heading rapidly in the same direction.

I continued to channel both my anger and my hope into activism of various kinds. From the late 1990s, I served as a representative for the Irish Seal Sanctuary at meetings for the North Atlantic Salmon Conservation Organisation (NASCO) in locations including Edinburgh, Glasgow, London, Paris, and even Quebec and Greenland. I was fortunate enough to have a certain amount of funding from the Seal Sanctuary to help with my travel costs, and I put the rest of the money in myself. I suppose that I was at a time in my life when I probably should have been thinking about my future and putting a little money away for my retirement, but I did not really give my own future that much thought. I was entirely preoccupied with the future of the Atlantic wild salmon and I considered that if I was able to make a difference, it was money and effort well spent.

Travelling to these meetings as a representative of the Seal Sanctuary was a strange position to be in, really. While NASCO was tasked with the urgent matter of addressing the rapid decline of salmon in the wild, many of its members were not sympathetic to the view that seals could and should be seen as part of a healthy, functioning ecosystem. The Irish Seal Sanctuary had identified seals as a population under threat in Ireland, while both Irish fishermen and Irish government authorities periodically claimed that problems with the salmon and other fish species populations were the result of seal predation.

At NASCO, I took a stance against the false premise that the seal population was largely to blame for the decline in salmon numbers. A lot of fishermen were still pointing accusing fingers at seals at that time, suggesting that they were entirely responsible for the crisis of salmon numbers. I doubt that anyone really believed that – anyone could see that a single trawler catch was more than an army of seals could consume over an extended period of time, while many seals also died after coming into contact with fishing trawlers. While some were still arguing for a seal cull, the Seal Sanctuary and I pointed out that the unfolding ecological disaster was entirely the fault of humans, not of animals whose populations would be in perfect balance with one another if left undisturbed.

The answer to the loss of one species should never be to attack another. Removing or drastically reducing the numbers of seals in the environment would have a complex knock-on effect on biodiversity in general, with unforeseeable results. We can draw some conclusions from the consequences of other examples of removing a species from the environment, or of drastically reducing its numbers.

Take, for instance, the case of myxomatosis. This disease exists in the wild in south and central America, where rabbits that catch it usually become only slightly unwell. It is a much more serious disease in European rabbits, which generally die very quickly after contracting it. The disease was introduced to Europe by French scientist Paul-Félix Armand-Delille – in order to protect his crop from rabbits, he released a pair infected with the Myxoma virus onto his farm in northern France.[136] It was deliberately introduced into the rabbit populations in Ireland and the UK in the 1950s to reduce their numbers, as they could do a lot of damage to crops and were widely considered to be a pest. I can still remember seeing diseased rabbits outside my national school, their poor heads swollen to three times their natural size.

My family ate a lot of fish and bacon, so we were fine, but in those days the rabbit was the poor man's dinner, and rural families all over Ireland suffered as the rabbit population fell. The intended consequence of the introduction of myxomatosis was the dramatic fall in the rabbit population that followed; unintended consequences included increased hardship for many country families that had depended on rabbit for protein in their diet, as well as a surge in attacks by foxes on domestic poultry, as their most obvious natural prey was now dying in vast numbers. There are numerous other examples of negative impacts of the destruction of species seen as simply inconvenient. It is just not possible to remove a species from its natural habitat without a rake of unintended consequences.

From 2000, I served on the National Salmon Commission, a body with about twenty-two members, all stakeholders in the world of salmon in various different ways. There were fish-buyers, anglers, owners of private fisheries, members of fishery boards and representatives of various groups of net-fishermen, as well as marine biologists and other industry professionals. At that time, the chairman of the Commission was Professor Noel Wilkins of NUI Galway, the marine scientist who had chaired the Task Force on Salmon Management. Noel was of the view that there were still abundant salmon in the Atlantic. I was drafted onto the Commission to represent traditional fishermen, partly, I believe, to give the impression that the authorities actually wanted to listen to people like me.

We had meetings all over the country – anywhere salmon were fished – and most of us participated in various subcommittees devoted to diverse related topics. I was involved, for example, in one that looked at seals. Of course, as usual, most of the other members were strongly in favour of a cull. It seemed so obvious to me that everyone was still desperately pointing their fingers at the seal, as they had been for years, because they simply did not want to believe the real story of colossal environmental mismanagement in fishing and hydroelectricity. I spent most of my time at those meetings in a state of outraged disbelief. I tried to get my message across, but it often felt as though I was just whistling into the wind.

Despite having been given the opportunity to participate in the Commission in a limited way, it seemed to me that the Commission's focus was not really on small-scale traditional fishermen at all, but on large trawlers. The atmosphere was very tense at most meetings, as competing interests failed to find common ground. Many people were pretending that we were not merely involved in a talking shop while one of the Atlantic's keystone species steadily moved towards extinction on our watch.

Frustrated by the lack of progress I was seeing, I drafted a questionnaire. It asked drift-net licence holders if they supported the concept of a buyout of their licences, and what sum they would regard as fair compensation. I circulated this, at my own expense, to about seven hundred and thirty of them. I signed the covering letter in my capacity as a drift-net fisherman and as a member of the National Salmon Commission and the subcommittee on 'incentivising reduction of commercial salmon fishing effort'.[137] The vast majority of people who responded stated that they were prepared to discuss the option of having their licences purchased from them as part of a buyout scheme. If this happened, a large number of people would have withdrawn permanently from fishing, and the money they received would have given them and their families some breathing space, and an opportunity to retrain and/or find new jobs in other sectors. It would, obviously, be easier for younger people to find work in new areas; for men in their fifties and sixties, who had been doing the same sort of work for many years, it would be much more difficult.

In response, Noel Wilkins stated his view that the proposed £100 million buyout of drift-net salmon fishing rights along the Atlantic seaboard was not supported by the government and was 'unworkable'. He claimed that such a move would encourage poaching on rivers and that it would be better to use consensus and conservation and encourage cooperation among anglers and commercial fishermen. It was obvious to me that this was not nearly enough, and I said so.

Now well known at the commission's meetings for my position that extinction was on the horizon for wild salmon, and that drastic measures were required to remedy the situation, I often found myself flanked by bulky security guards, as though I posed some sort of physical threat to other delegates. But I really was not saying anything controversial or extreme: in July 2000, an *Irish Times* editorial pointed out that Ireland and Britain were the only North Atlantic countries that had not taken decisive steps towards ending drift netting. Iceland, Norway and the Faroe Islands had all made significant changes, and Ireland and Britain's failure to follow suit was now understandably causing bad feeling – those nations felt that they were conserving stocks in their waters only for them to be taken by trawlers working off the Irish and British coasts.[138]

Amid a lot of bad feeling on all sides, Professor Wilkins retired from the commission in 2001.[139] He was replaced by Joey Murrin, who had started out as a deckhand on a fishing boat, and had served as chair of Bord Iascaigh Mhara from 1986. Joey was a gifted organiser and a fiercely intelligent man. He was a passionate advocate for fishermen to a fault, but I felt he should have paid more attention to the wider picture, which was that unless the fish populations were also supported, before too long there would not even be any fishermen.

A quota system was agreed, but the quotas for salmon actually far exceeded the number of salmon available. Even without the widespread poaching that continued, it would have been a further step towards the extinction of the species. Because illegal fishing continued unabated, it was actually much worse.

By now, I had been involved in activism on the behalf of estuary net-fishermen for two decades. I had travelled all over Ireland speaking to men who had worked in fishing all their lives, and who had never seen the sort of devastation that we were becoming so familiar with now. We all knew that our traditional way of life was essentially over unless something truly dramatic happened to change everything.

All I wanted at this stage was to raise awareness. It was clear to me that the numbers of wild salmon were now well below sustainability, unless drastic action were taken. I did my best to get the message out. In 2002, a journalist, Ted O'Riordan, interviewed me about a website I had set up to promote the concept of a complete ban on drift-net fishing. Reading it now, I remember how upset I was about the unfolding ecological disaster, and also how determined I was to get people to listen to me. Ted quoted me describing drift nets as 'walls of death', which caught enormous numbers of fish, most of which were not even wanted and were swiftly thrown back into the ocean. Almost all of these were dead by the time they were returned to the water. It was an absolutely colossal waste.[140]

In 2003, of twelve fishing licences issued in Coonagh, only three boats were actually going out fishing, and they were catching almost nothing. That same year, Orri Vigfússon and I met Eamon Ryan TD, then the Green Party spokesperson for Transport, Enterprise, Trade and Employment, Communications, Marine and Natural Resources. He said all the right things at first, but Fianna Fáil and the Progressive Democrats were in power at the time, so there was little he could do. It also quickly became very clear that Eamon knew almost nothing about the life cycle of the salmon, the complex reasons why its future was in doubt, and the roles that Irish hydroelectricity and overfishing at sea were having in its looming demise.

Shortly after our meeting with Eamon, the newspapers were full of the latest scandal involving salmon farming – large numbers of salmon carcasses had been stuffed into bags and buried in a bog in Casla in

Connemara, following a massive die-off at the salmon farm. The salmon farm in question was owned by John O'Carroll, director of the Irish Seafood Producers Group – the largest salmon export company in Ireland at that time. John owned a salmon farm in the Connemara Gaeltacht, and was also a board member of the Marine Institute, a State agency with an environmental remit.

Given the copious quantities of rotting salmon in that Connemara bog, there were concerns that the local water supply would be affected. The then Minister of the Marine, Dermot Ahern of Fianna Fáil, said that he had been assured by his staff that the regulation, inspection and investigation regime in the salmon farming sector was 'rigorous'. For anyone looking on, it seemed that the whole salmon industry was just about as rotten as those bags of dumped fish.[141] The dump of rotting fish was a disgrace, and so was the lack of care and due diligence given to a complex industry and a very vulnerable keystone species.

New regulations stated that nobody should use a boat over forty feet long for salmon-fishing, but the well-connected were not only using boats of sixty or seventy or a hundred feet, they were getting government grants to buy them. I had grown used to hearing and participating in what might be called robust exchanges of views at meetings about fishing and fishing rights and who was allowed to do what, but now such meetings were often deeply unpleasant. People representing conflicting views would shout at each other and issue threats. Occasional scuffles would even break out, and people had to be physically separated.

That was bad enough, but it was not as bad as the fear you might feel on leaving a meeting alongside a large number of angry people with competing interests. So long as everyone was contained in a meeting room, there was a limit to how violent things were going to get. Outside and away from view, it could be another matter. We had all heard terrible stories of threats, intimidation and violence. It was hard not to be scared.

CHAPTER NINE

Too Late and Not Enough

By the 2000s, the salmon available for sale in supermarkets was very different to the salmon of earlier times. Now that farmed salmon was embedded into food supply chains, people had grown used to it. The meat came from stressed fish raised in crowded, unhealthy conditions. Many of the farmed fish were weakened by parasites such as sea lice and other diseases. Because of their poor muscle tone, the flesh was flabby and soft and almost fell apart in your hands. For those who really knew the wild salmon, and how it should taste and feel, it was practically inedible, revolting even. But for those who knew no better, the supermarket fish was a cheap source of protein, often considered 'healthier' than other types of meat. For those who were leaning towards vegetarianism and squeamish about eating meat like beef, lamb and pork, farmed fish seemed to offer a middle ground. Nobody ever felt sorry for factory-farmed fish the way they did for calves being raised for veal.

Farmed salmon was a very big business – and it was also a cop-out, seen by the powers that be as easier than addressing the serious problems that

Ireland and other countries had with pollution and the mismanagement of the fisheries. In 2001, the World Wildlife Fund (WWF) reported that wild salmon were now extinct in 11 per cent of Irish rivers and were critically endangered in many more. While that was dreadful enough, the WWF also reported that things were even worse elsewhere. Worldwide, the stock of salmon had fallen by 80 per cent, and 90 per cent of the known healthy population was in a small area including Ireland, Iceland and Norway.[142]

It was no longer possible for those in power to pretend that there was no problem. But stakeholders in the fish-farming industry, and others, continued to argue about what constituted a 'wild' fish. Some maintained that any fish that engaged in a migratory pattern and returned to spawn could be considered 'wild', even if it originated in a hatchery or had escaped from a farm.[143] By maintaining that these fish – which would not exist but for human intervention – were 'wild', they managed to deflect attention from the environmental disaster taking place.

I was still hopeful that if the authorities really understood what was going on, perhaps steps might be taken to protect the Atlantic wild salmon. I felt that the North Atlantic Salmon Fund was its best chance. By this stage, the fund, led by Orri Vigfússon, had succeeded on a number of fronts: through strategic buyouts and political reforms, salmon netting in the Atlantic was reduced. In 1991 and 1995, it had brokered moratoriums on fishing off the Faroe Islands, the location of the feeding grounds of the wild salmon of Norway.

When we met for the first time, I had been unconvinced by Orri's position that a complete cessation of salmon fishing was needed. Gradually, I had come to accept that he was right. Now I could see that this really was the salmon's only chance. From 2001, I was directly involved in Orri's

North Atlantic Salmon Fund. My role was to represent Orri on the ground in Ireland, communicating with interested parties, organising meetings and getting his message out. I travelled all over the country, visiting fishing communities and organising events at which a practical way forward that had the potential to save the Atlantic wild salmon, while also fairly compensating fishermen, was discussed. We still had a genuine chance to save the salmon from extinction, and I felt that it was worth it.

Every single fisherman in Ireland was given the opportunity to meet and speak with Orri, though not all of them were interested. It was as though they were competing to see who would be the one to catch the last wild salmon. Meeting all of these people, speaking to them about their concerns and trying to get my point of view across, I could not help but notice that the age profile of fishermen was skewed significantly upwards. Younger people had seen the writing on the wall and very few of them were interested in going into the industry.

Driving grimly up and down the country roads of Ireland, on what felt like an increasingly damned-to-fail quest to save the salmon, I could see how our entire relationship with the natural world had been utterly transformed. Farming in my youth had involved machinery like tractors, ploughs and harrows and threshing machines, but it had still relied heavily on the labour of people prepared to get their hands dirty. By the twenty-first century, farms had increasingly been consolidated into larger units, with hedgerows ripped out and agriculture approached as an industrial enterprise. I was sure we were losing as many species on land as we were in the water. I did not let myself think about it. It was hard enough trying to save the salmon, without worrying about all the other endangered species too.

By 2003, researchers in America had determined that State efforts to restore salmon to rivers in the Atlantic region had failed, and that the Atlantic wild salmon had effectively disappeared from North American rivers.[144] The exact same story was playing out all over the Atlantic region, but some of us were still fighting against a fate that looked increasingly inevitable. That year, following a number of buyouts in various parts of the Atlantic region, the North Atlantic Salmon Fund was attempting a buyout of drift nets in Ireland, alongside investment in inshore fishing and alternative fisheries. The idea was both to conserve the salmon and to provide alternative forms of employment so that small communities could thrive.

Together with others who understood and agreed with Orri's approach, I did my best to get the same crucial message across: if we were serious about the survival of the Atlantic wild salmon, we had to let go of the idea that conservation measures could be taken alongside maintaining the salmon fishery. It was far too late for that. The only hope for the species was a ban on drift netting for as long as it took for numbers to rebound. The situation was so urgent, and so important to me personally, that I travelled the country with the zeal of an evangelist. I attended meetings, held meetings about arranging other meetings, and told everyone I could that the end times for the salmon were approaching and that we needed to act now.

Much of this travel, with the associated costs of accommodation and food, was funded from my own pocket, at the same time as my income from fishing was declining. I did not have access to the sort of funds that the likes of Orri might, but like him, I realised that if I was serious, I needed to put my money where my mouth was. So I did. I spent all the money I had bar what I needed for the basic necessities of life.

Mam, in her late eighties now, did everything she could to help. She had supported me through good times and bad in my fishing career, and now that I was predominantly involved in activism, she was tirelessly helpful. She answered the phone, committed messages to memory and relayed them to me when I got home.

By 2004, there was a little good news. It seemed that those countries that had severely restricted the drift netting of salmon were seeing a modest change for the better. That year, there was decisive evidence from Iceland that salmon numbers were up, in the form of the best angling season in at least twenty-five years. Orri Vigfússon was quoted as saying that the last year the runs had been as good was 1978.[145]

Also in 2004, most members of the Irish Salmon Netmen's Association, of which I was then chairman, accepted the need to stop fishing for a while. They were prepared to have their salmon-netting rights purchased and to temporarily retire from fishing in exchange for modest amounts of compensation, about eighty thousand euro per licence.[146] That would give them some breathing space to retrain if necessary and find other ways to support their families.

It was a very difficult situation for men who were middle-aged and older. They might have been fishing for thirty or forty years, and realistically the chance of their finding decent work in another field was slight. There was pushback in some quarters, from those who did not see why the fishermen should get any compensation at all. Some argued that they had chosen to go into fishing; they had caused the situation themselves through overfishing; and now they should just deal with the destruction of their livelihoods on their own.

But the fishermen were not a sealed system; they were part of the broader economy. There was little to be gained from punishing the smaller actors in the field at a particularly difficult time in their lives, while many boats owned by wealthy businessmen were straying hundreds of kilometres from the fishing grounds where they were allowed to work to other areas, in search of salmon on their way home to spawn. People from diverse backgrounds were travelling all the way along the salmon migratory route – invading remote fishing areas and greedily intercepting fish far from their home rivers – in the hope of obtaining big catches of salmon migrating from the feeding grounds.

At sea, illegal fishing continued, and not just of salmon. In 2004, a Garda investigation, involving more than a hundred gardaí, raided trawlers, factories where fish was processed and other businesses in the Atlantic coast area.[147] They uncovered that Irish trawlers had been 'routinely and systematically' exceeding their daily fish quotas by up to ten times the limits set by the European Union, while recording different sorts of fish being caught than were actually being caught.

The further the fishing grounds were from the urban centres where civil servants and State bodies were located, the easier it was for fishermen to flout the conditions of their licences, taking their boats far beyond the six-mile limit that was supposed to contain fishing within a certain distance of the ports they worked out of. In some areas, there was simply no rule of law in any functional way. It was a slap in the face to those generational fishermen who did not have big money behind them and who had always fished within the limits.

By 2005, the National Salmon Commission wound up most of its activities after a five-year session. It was reconstituted for a second session, but this lasted for less than a year. I had pulled out after the first session. It was a time of change for me in more ways than one, because Mam had died in March of that year, aged ninety-one. She had been well, engaged with the community and positive until the end. How blessed I was to have been able to be so close to her. I was sixty-two years old at that time – nearing retirement age myself, had I wanted or been able to retire – so I had been very fortunate to have her for so long. Mam was a wonderful mother to all her children. As a younger woman, she had worked her fingers to the bone caring for and providing for us. All though my years of coming and going from London, she was there for me. We buried her with Dad in Mount Saint Lawrence Cemetery in Limerick. She had outlived him by thirty years, and had seen as much – if not more – social change during her widowhood as she had during their entire married life. They were together again at last.

In 2006, research showed that only 43 per cent of Irish salmon rivers reached their conservation limits – the spawning stock level below which the number of salmon entering the population declines significantly.[148] The Irish government finally banned the drift netting of wild salmon, in a desperate attempt to save the species, which by this stage had been in decline for at least eight decades – not just in Ireland, but everywhere across the region.

The ban was long overdue. The modern drift nets, in general usage since the 1960s, had been disastrous for the environment, and they still were now. In fact, they were even worse. The materials they were made of were stronger now than ever, and the depths they could reach had doubled, or even trebled. They caught enormous numbers of the fish that the fishermen were looking for, but also snagged large numbers of other species, which then died entirely needlessly. When drift nets got lost at sea, which inevitably happened quite often, they remained undegraded for years, and could damage vast amounts of wildlife that simply swam into them and were unable to escape. Bear in mind that these drift nets were absolutely enormous. A net measuring thousands of square metres was capable of doing terrible damage, even when it was no longer associated with a trawler and was simply floating around in the open ocean by itself.

In 2007, for example, a dead basking shark was washed up in Brandon Bay, having become entangled in a drift net.[149] For the fishermen who used them, before and after the ban, the drift nets represented a considerable expense, and of course it was very frustrating for them when they were damaged or lost. Consequently, when undesired species became entangled in drift nets that were still attached to trawlers, the crew typically responded brutally.

Basking sharks are a benign species that represent no threat to human beings. Because they live on zooplankton, they also represent no threat to salmon or other species consumed by humans. But, of course, if they are tangled in a net, they will panic and try to get free, and because they are large creatures they are capable of doing a lot of damage. To neutralise the threat they posed to the net, and to the day's fishing it contained, when they became entangled, fishermen would often haul them alongside the boat and cut off their tails. This left them largely unable to move and they would lie there – presumably in dreadful pain – while they were untangled, after which they would sink to the bottom of the sea to suffer a terrible death. The same thing happened to dolphins.

Guillemots, birds that spend most of their lives at sea and only come to shore during the breeding season, also frequently became entangled in nets, and were generally summarily removed by cutting the wings off the living birds and tossing them into the sea to perish. Another species that could get tangled in nets and was often slaughtered was the fishermen's favourite scapegoat, the seal.

The government decided to compensate those most badly affected by the drift-net ban. In 2006, an Independent Salmon Group was established to advise the government on the implications of adhering to the scientific advice issued by bodies such as NASCO, including the hardships and financial difficulties of those who had depended on salmon fishing. Its advice was simple: the government needed to take drastic measures to stop the terminal decline of salmon in Irish waters.[150] After consulting with various stakeholders, it recommended that the government should issue hardship payments based on the recent catch history of the fishermen holding licences. The system would be managed by Bord Iascaigh Mhara, the Irish Fisheries Board, and regional fisheries boards.

On paper it all looked okay, but as so often happens in Ireland, the system was badly designed, badly executed and riddled with corruption. Most of the money from the hardship fund went to those who had lodged the biggest catches, with their own logbooks submitted as evidence. Legislation intended to prevent poaching post-receipt of hardship funds was put in place, but never enforced. It was essentially a compensation scheme for the wealthy, many of whom had already intimidated small-scale fishermen out of the business that had supported them and their forebears throughout history.

Agitators blamed the decline in fish on foreign trawlers working in Irish waters – and they were certainly part of the problem – but this ignored the fact that domestic boats were fishing just as recklessly, while also getting 'compensation' from the State.

On 26 October 2006, I wrote to Noel Dempsey, then the Minister of the Marine. I drew his attention to a public statement I had made, suggesting he should invite Orri Vigfússon to Ireland to help broker a compensation scheme for those who held salmon net-licences. Orri could address hardship more fairly by equally compensating all those who were losing out. I wanted to see fishermen from small inland fisheries compensated in the same manner as those running huge trawlers, and suggested that a flat sum of €200,000 would make it possible for people to retrain, find work or set up alternative businesses. There was considerable media coverage, but as I lacked the political clout of the wealthy trawler-owners, this never happened. Generational fisherman, taking in quite small catches using broadly traditional techniques, were largely left to fend for themselves, while owners of enormous trawlers and big enterprises received massive compensation, despite having made millions contributing to bringing the Atlantic salmon to the edge of extinction.

By this time, the tourist fishing business was also floundering. For generations, anglers from all over the world had visited Ireland to fish for salmon using rods, hooks and lures in the rivers. As a migrating salmon effectively has to be persuaded to take a lure, this is a highly skilled occupation and it resulted in the capture of few fish relative to the vast numbers being hauled onto trawlers. Anglers for salmon did not expect to catch many fish, but they did need to feel that they were in with a chance of one or two.

By 2006, the year when the Irish government was advised to cease drift netting entirely, there were so few wild salmon left in the rivers that many anglers were no longer visiting the Shannon.[151] But the authorities at the time were apparently largely uninterested in conserving stocks.[152]

The drift-net ban had come years too late, and it was now enforced haphazardly at best by the Fisheries Board. Some illegal drift nets were identified and confiscated – such as one that measured more than one and a half miles long, seized off the coast in the autumn of 2007.[153] But this was far too little, far too late. It seemed to me that the ban was really nothing more than window dressing. Of course, some fishermen flouted it, and when the authorities apprehended them, they were prosecuted and given derisory fines, and were allowed to escape the mandatory penalty of forfeiture of compensation.

Attitudes towards poachers varied considerably within the fishing industry. Some people saw them as cute fellas who were getting one over on the State and fair play to them, while others were angry that they were continuing to take from a stock of fish that was more depleted with each day that passed.

But even this illegal overfishing was only a small part of the reason for the near-extinction of the Atlantic wild salmon. It now took double the number of eggs to produce a single, healthy adult salmon that would return to its natal river to spawn,[154] compared to the period before 1990, when the situation was already utterly dreadful. And the fact was that by far the biggest owner of the salmon fisheries was the State itself, through its agencies the ESB, the Fisheries Board and the Wildlife Service. In other words, if the State was truly serious about saving the salmon, it could easily have taken steps to do so.

Meanwhile, other species experiencing similar situations to the salmon were also coming under the radar of conservationists and policymakers. In 2007, for example, the European eel – *Anguilla anguilla* – was listed on Appendix II of the Convention on International Trade in Endangered Species.[155] One of the primary reasons for the dramatic drop in numbers was river-engineering works, which destroyed the habitats of juvenile eels. In Ireland, because of the Ardnacrusha power station, eels were unable to reach their habitats. They could only survive if young eels were rescued in nets and transported upstream, bypassing the station.

The same year, the State Fisheries Protection Association was founded under the provisions of the Sea-Fisheries and Maritime Jurisdiction Act 2006, working for the Department of Agriculture, Food and the Marine. It was supposed to oversee the enforcement of the law where it applies to sea fisheries and seafood, and report to the minister. Whether or not it would make any difference was a matter of debate.

The people who knew the Shannon best – the fishermen – could see how the decline of wild salmon was impacting on other species too. Once, for example, the waters had been rich in freshwater mussels, whose seeds had previously been carried by the salmon and other wild fish. Now their numbers, too, were in precipitous decline. With fewer small fish to eat, there were fewer waterbirds. The ripple effect of the poor management of the salmon was damaging every corner of the freshwater ecosystem, including the rural communities that once worked in harmony with it. And yet politicians and far too many of the 'experts' involved in planning for the future of fishing all too often supported policies that exacerbated an already dire situation, prioritising short-term profit over long-term gain.

In 2010, the Irish government passed the Inland Fisheries Act, and the Inland Fisheries Ireland organisation was established to protect, manage and conserve Ireland's inland fisheries and sea-angling resources. I was cautiously optimistic initially that the organisation would be willing to engage with fishermen like me, but it soon became apparent that there was a very clear 'us and them'. There was very little respect among the employees of the organisation for fishermen, who might not have higher degrees in marine biology but who had been working with fish all their lives.

By 2012, research showed that, among other challenges, Irish salmon were no longer growing at sea the way they did before. Earlier research, from 1963 to 1981, had shown that salmon in those years had grown quickly during their first year at sea. Now, for reasons that were not entirely clear, they were growing much less, and also surviving in much smaller numbers.[156] Could it be coincidental that wild salmon were, during this period, being replaced by ranched fish that had been born in hatcheries, while at the same time rates of disease were increasing rapidly, in great part as a result of intensive fish farming?

The authorities maintained that sea louse infestations did not have a dramatic impact on the health of wild salmon. However, the Irish Marine Institute inspections of fish farms in accordance with laws laid out by the Department of Agriculture, Food and the Marine according to its Monitoring Protocol (established in 2000) and its Strategy (published in 2008),[157] suggested that they were well aware of the problems with sea lice. Smolts, whether wild or released from hatcheries, left their natal rivers and passed right by salmon farms on their way out to the Atlantic and their feeding grounds in the waters of Greenland. In the process, many of them picked up sea lice from heavily infested farmed populations. These same smolts now had to travel to their feeding grounds and try to grow and thrive despite hosting unnatural quantities of parasites. Of course, large numbers of them failed to thrive and died, and others clung to life but did not grow as they should have.

Another factor in the decline of salmon, also related to the artificial hatchery environment in which so many now started their lives, was the dramatically reduced genetic diversity in the salmon population. In order to adapt to an ever-changing environment, the genetic diversity of the salmon needed to be preserved,[158] but this was not happening.

By 2016, the already-depleted salmon population had declined by a further 33 per cent as compared to 1990. Now, it was estimated that there were just 3.38 million wild salmon left.[159]

According to the United Nations, a wild game species – like the Atlantic salmon – is entitled to protection, largely because it is seen as a food source for the population of the world. Each member state of the United Nations is supposed to support these species. Most of them have got very good at pretending they have a regulated, healthy system that supports wild populations. Where there are problems, most blame everything on factors largely outside their individual control, such as climate change. They generally ignore the effects of new fishing technologies. The reality is that the decline in salmon is a direct result of their compromised habitat, largely because of hydroelectric dams; because of badly executed legislation around salmon fishing and salmon farming; and – ultimately – because of the massive levels of corruption that ensure that those in authority continue to look the other way.

Instead of tackling the root of the problem, special interests such as fish farms have looked for creative ways to address the issues they are facing. The extraordinary levels of parasite infestation witnessed in salmon farms, which should be read as a clear indication that they are not the way to go, have instead inspired the use of fish such as wild ballan and wrasse, which consume sea lice, in the hope that they will make the farmed salmon population healthier by reducing the numbers of lice.[160] When these wild fish have completed this task, they are killed and discarded rather than released back into the wild.

Yes, salmon farmers are actually capturing wild fish and placing them inside salmon farms to improve the compromised health of the parasite-infested salmon. The inevitable consequence is that they are now endangering the sustainability of populations of ballan and wrasse too.

In 2018, a 'working group' was formed, comprising local stakeholders, representatives from government departments and the ESB, to look at improving the fish passages through Ardnacrusha power station and Parteen Weir.[161] About ninety years too late, it was difficult to take it seriously, given that one of the major partners – the ESB – had a vested interest in the status quo.

Meanwhile, many sea fishermen continued – even after all these years, and in the face of the scientific evidence – to insist that seals were to blame for the massive decline in salmon numbers. Feelings ran high. Because I had been outspoken on the matter of the seals, I even received an anonymous letter, presumably from an angry fisherman: 'Great news,' it said, 'seals being strangled in their thousands … with new gear, ha ha ha …'

Also in 2018, Irish Water took advantage of a drought to build numerous weirs across twenty-three Irish rivers, resulting in mass die-offs of fish, although officialdom stated that the weirs had been inspected by Inland Fisheries Ireland, which saw no problem with them.

Ireland is failing dismally at protecting its keystone species, and so is everybody else. In 2019, the United Nations Food and Agriculture Organisation revealed that over 35 per cent of fish populations were being extracted at levels that are unsustainable.[162] That same year, NASCO reported that, of 2359 rivers in the North Atlantic area studied, only 341, or 14 per cent, were considered to still have sustainable salmon populations.[163]

In some cases, efforts to replenish depleted stocks with ranched fish made matters worse in ways that could not have been foreseen. For instance, it emerged that male salmon raised in captivity were much less successful than wild males at courting, competing for access to females and successful spawning.[164] After all these years, it was now abundantly clear that being raised in captivity simply did not prepare them for the demands of the natural environment. If a female attempted to breed with one of these captive-raised males, her eggs were less likely to be fertilised, and an opportunity to contribute to the next generation of salmon could be lost.

By 2019, about 20 per cent of the world's total catch of wild fish was being processed into fishmeal and fish oil, mostly for the fish-farming industry,[165] with about 60 per cent of the fish oil used in aquaculture going to feed salmon and trout.[166] Feeding farmed salmon is unsustainable over the long term, as it takes about three pounds of other wild fish species to grow a farmed salmon's weight by one pound. Much of this wild fish is harvested in poor countries, and then used to feed farmed fish that will end up on the table in wealthy countries. So, while it may support local industry in the developing world, it may also impact negatively on diets there, while contributing to a farmed-fish industry that is proving to threaten the entire marine environment.

In 2020, the European Court of Auditors reported that the European Union was not doing enough to protect its oceans and allow them to restock, despite the policies it had put in place.[167] In 2023, Norwegian research showed that the numbers of salmon returning to Norway each year to spawn was less than half those recorded in the 1990s. The same picture could be seen everywhere across the entire North Atlantic region.[168]

By this stage, global warming had become a convenient scapegoat on which all the problems of the marine environment could be blamed. Of course, global warming is a real and serious threat to the environment. But the extent to which it is damaging populations such as the Atlantic wild salmon is unknown, while the dreadful situation caused by hydroelectricity, overfishing and salmon farming has been thoroughly researched. We are now seeing interested parties using the spectre of global warming as a convenient smokescreen. It can disguise the fact that their own activities cause much more, and much more fully researched damage, and have been doing so for years. If it was not all so tragic, you would have to laugh.

In my seventies now, I had a growing sense of urgency about the work I was doing. It looked as though the Atlantic wild salmon was not going to be around for much longer. As my own peers and friends started to become frail and leave the fight, I had to face the unpalatable fact that I would not be around forever myself. I was still working – a little bit of fishing, but mostly reed-cutting for a few clients with thatched homes – and still had my hobbies and interests, which included playing bridge, flying light aircraft and hanging around the airfield to talk to the like-minded. But my main preoccupation as I faced into what are euphemistically referred to as the golden years was, as ever, the salmon.

By now, I had dedicated decades of my life to the salmon – my whole life, really, from the day I was old enough to understand where Dad was going in his gandelow, and to decide that I wanted to go with him. I had fished for salmon, eaten salmon and seen the salmon's numbers decline as a result of the North Atlantic region's long experiment with hydroelectricity and the chronic overfishing of its seas and estuaries. I had attended countless meetings, given countless interviews and had innumerable conversations, always trying to get across my message that the beautiful wild salmon, a cornerstone of the traditional diet of the various peoples of the North Atlantic region, a wondrous creature memorialised in song and legend, would soon be no more.

I realised that I needed to find a new way to get my message out, one that would reach a larger number of people and communicate with them in a different sort of way. I decided to write a book. Perhaps, I thought, if people understood what the Shannon had been like once – when I was little, and long before that; before Ardnacrusha was built, before the pollution was as bad as it is today, before the salmon was on the verge of extinction – they would be more open to listening to a plan that I have been working on for years. A plan that, I believe, has the potential to transform the fate of the Atlantic wild salmon and, in the process, make our waters better for everyone.

Well, I thought, as I started to write, *you never know. Perhaps it'll work. Nothing else has, so it's worth a shot.*

CHAPTER TEN

The Plan

The Atlantic wild salmon is, at the time of writing, functionally extinct. We are facing the end of a species that has been fundamental not just to Irish communities, but to communities all around the North Atlantic, literally since prehistory. If we continue along our current path, it will not be long before it is gone forever, and with it a profound link between us, the natural environment around us and our most remote human ancestors.

When I was at school, I loved learning about history and geography, because the idea that we have to know about the past to understand the present made sense to me. I also grew up in a very traditional rural community, in which the past often seemed to coexist with the present, such was the detail with which old stories were told by our parents and grandparents. They could speak about times long before any of them were born with the same keenness and detail that you would find in the dissection of a hurling final in the pub after the game.

As an adult, I still had this fascination with the past, and made a point of reading books about history whenever I could, attending lectures and building on my knowledge of the old days. Doing this has brought a great depth to my life and to how I see and understand the issues of today.

The Irish government, and governments and business interests in many other jurisdictions, have invested heavily – financially and emotionally – in the idea of raising salmon populations by introducing artificially raised fish. This practice has been ongoing in some parts of the world for over a hundred years, and in recent decades, production has ramped up to an incredible degree. Ranched salmon and salmon farming constitute major threats to the way of life of communities that have fished on a small scale and in a sustainable way for generations, like the Inuit people of Greenland and the Irish fishermen of Coonagh, County Limerick.

The Irish government has neglected to address the fact that hydroelectricity is extremely damaging to the environment. Instead, it continues to throw money at it. In 2022, the Irish government passed legislation permitting hydroelectrical works to extract water for power-generation purposes without carrying out proper ecological assessments first.[169] As we have previously seen, hydroelectricity has been given free rein since its beginnings in Ireland shortly after the foundation of the State; the 1925 Shannon Electricity Act wrote into the law that fish would only be protected if this was not inconvenient for electricity production. This is the spirit in which the modern laws are still being interpreted. In 2023, up to 90 per cent of the flow of the entire River Shannon was diverted at the Parteen Weir, all to provide just 2 per cent of the country's electricity needs. At that time, the Inland Fisheries Ireland organisation was in a state of profound disarray, the remnants of what had once been its management board disbanded.[170]

Yet, despite years of neglect, there is still a glimmer of hope that the numbers of salmon could grow again – and I have a plan that could really work. We can still save Ireland's most iconic indigenous species and revitalise rural communities, giving them a future and retaining their links to the past. We do not need enquiries or surveys, or consultations with special-interest groups, because it is already too late for all of that. Other plans have failed to address the issue because they were too little, too late. It is time for a drastic approach, and there is no time to wait.

We need to make some bold moves that will be, at one and the same time, a large-scale scientific experiment into how to repair a badly damaged ecosystem; and the Atlantic wild salmon's last chance at survival.

It involves just six steps, which are simple – if not easy. My modest proposal is as follows:

FIRST STEP: CLOSE THE SALMON RIVERS TO FISHING

All fishing for wild fish should be closed across the entire western seaboard of Europe for a period of at least ten years. Equivalent areas in the Americas can remain open to fishing during the same period, while the Americas continue with business as usual. This will provide researchers with a robust set of data that can be used in forward planning. At the moment, scientists and policy-formers have no choice but to make major decisions on the basis of assumption and flawed data. I am sure that at least some of them are doing their best, but in the current state of crisis, that is not nearly enough.

Closing all fishing for wild salmon across the entire western seaboard of Europe will call for massive, even unprecedented, levels of international cooperation. To save a species that roams across a vast, shared area, we will need the help and input of diplomats, departments of the marine, fishermen, universities and more. We will need a unified body to coordinate all of their efforts. My suggestion is that the United Nations could step in and provide the administrative structure that will be required.

Someone has to make the first step, so why not Ireland? As the European Union's most westerly nation, with the wide Atlantic Ocean all that there is between us and the Americas, perhaps we can bring a proposal to the table, and get the rest of the Atlantic nations to run with it.

SECOND STEP: CLOSE THE HATCHERIES

The salmon hatcheries were opened with good intentions – to produce smolts to populate the salmon rivers. After all these years, though, we are stuck in a sunk-cost fallacy. So much effort, money, time, emotion and reputation have been invested in the hatcheries that it is difficult to accept that, in the longer run, they have done more damage than good. They will continue to do so if they are left open.

When the hatcheries have been closed for just two or three years, we will have much more accurate information about how many wild salmon there truly are, and how viable their population actually is, as the ranched salmon – which have a much lower successful reproduction rate – will be fished out and will steadily die of natural causes.

Obviously, without hatcheries, there can be no fish farms. Salmon fish farms cannot survive without a constant supply of young fish to grow. Since salmon farming became large scale and widespread, it has been an immense hazard to the continued existence of the Atlantic wild salmon. As we have seen, the disease and infestations that emanate from salmon farms and enter the wild population are a huge problem, but that is not all. There is very little genetic diversity among farmed-salmon populations. When there are large numbers of escapees, inevitably they breed with wild salmon, which are now breeding from within a much narrower genetic pool, without the diversity that they need to thrive. By closing down salmon farms completely, we will be giving the wild salmon a fighting chance.

People eat so much farmed salmon these days that it may seem difficult to imagine a diet without it, but people can and will adapt. While there are many arguments in favour of a vegan or vegetarian diet, in my view it is unrealistic to expect the majority of people to completely drop meat and fish from their diets. Most of us could stand to reduce the amount of fish and animal protein in our diets, however. There are various species of fish that can be farmed at far less cost to the environment. Inland non-migratory fish, which do not require salt water, can be farmed in enclosed tanks located away from natural watercourses. These could replace salmon.

THIRD STEP: IMPROVE THE EFFICIENCY OF FISH PASSES FOR RETURNING FISH

Next, all weirs and industrial infrastructure on rivers and waterways across the entire North Atlantic region must be significantly upgraded. It needs to be much, much easier for fish to cross these obstacles and make their way to their spawning grounds. At the moment, salmon and other species are often expected to travel upriver by means of water cascading down artificially created steps, or fish passes. While it is possible for fish to traverse these passes, and some of them do, they are a significant obstacle to the safe passage of the fish upstream. The main problem on the Shannon, for example, is the lack of water flow. Here, taking water out of the head race to use in the existing fish passes instead would make it much easier for the fish to navigate the passes.

Think of it from their point of view: by the time they reach the fish pass, they are already exhausted. They have not been eating for a while, and they have just one thing on their minds – the burning need to get back to where they came from to spawn. Confronted with a set of steps to swim up, and often an inadequate water supply to do so, as is the situation on the Shannon, they frequently manage to leap up several, only to eventually give up from exhaustion. They might even reach the top, but then find their energy levels so depleted that their capacity to swim further is compromised.

On some rivers, it can sometimes be possible to create a bypass river. This is a looped canal constructed around obstacles, a low-gradient waterway that is easy for the fish to manage. This sort of technology is not new, startling or innovative, and bypasses of this nature are already in place in some areas of the North Atlantic.

The technology involved is very simple, so why are bypass rivers not constructed all the time? While sometimes the natural features of the land-scape inhibit the possibility, often it comes down to money. Infrastructure of this sort calls for the compulsory purchase of land adjacent to the main river, a huge amount of labour and a great deal of expense. However, with modern digging and other technologies, it is much more realisable than it was in the past, when work was carried out by labourers with picks, shovels and brute strength. The environmental gains are potentially enormous.

FOURTH STEP: CLEAR THE WAY FOR THE WILD SALMON

As things stand, wild salmon, with a life span of not more than six years, are forced to compete for resources with ranched fish, escapees from salmon farms and hybrids. By removing the competition in a measured and orderly manner, we can create space for the wild salmon to feed, spawn and grow as a population. Through the steady fishing-out of ranched fish, the elim-ination of hatcheries and the rapid construction of means for wild fish to bypass obstacles along waterways, the truly wild salmon will be given space to grow, live and reproduce.

FIFTH STEP: CLOSE DOWN THE COMMERCIAL FISHERY IN GREENLAND

We will need to work hand in hand with international partners to address major issues. At the time of writing, the devastating commercial fishery in the waters of Greenland is taking so many salmon out of the system – the few remaining wild salmon and hatchery salmon from all over the Atlantic region alike – that, even if all the steps above were enacted all across the North Atlantic region, it would not be enough.

Huge diplomacy will be required to vastly reduce fishing off the coast of Greenland, while also protecting the rights of the indigenous Greenlanders, who are quite few in number and should be allowed to take what they personally need, while the large commercial fishing fleets are decommissioned.

Greenland is the feeding ground for salmon from all over the Atlantic. What happens there impacts on the entire region, and there is no way around it: we will all need to work together to cease commercial salmon fishing in the waters of Greenland.

SIXTH STEP: UNBLOCK THE RIVERS

We need to see the immediate decommissioning of non-productive power stations and dams that are no longer economic or fit for purpose, and their replacement with natural river courses and flows.

Here in Ireland, what of the Ardnacrusha power station and all of the ancillary works and constructions associated with it? Well, once everything that is an impediment to the safe passage of salmon and other keystone species has been removed from the Shannon, we can use all that is left in a new way. We in Ireland can take a leadership role by starting with the decommissioning of the Parteen Weir and Ardnacrusha hydroelectric plant. We must halt, and remove, the huge turbines in the station, and eliminate all dams.

The power station itself is one of Ireland's most important examples of industrial architecture, and it should certainly be preserved. The tail race and other elements of the infrastructure could be repurposed for sporting and recreational activities. In a matter of just a few years, the Ardnacrusha power station and the entire Shannon area could cease damaging the delicate balance of our environment and could, instead, become a beacon of hope for the future. Similar enterprises could be established everywhere there are hydroelectric plants.

While most countries in the North Atlantic region continue to use old-fashioned hydroelectric plants, where dams have been removed, the evidence shows that salmon populations do start to rebound. For example, in Maine in the United States, the removal of two dams from the Penobscot River, and the construction of a river-like bypass around a third large dam, significantly improved access for salmon and other migratory species.[171]

Before I am accused of zealotry, let me stress than I am in no way a technophobe. On the contrary, I have always had a huge interest in and love of machinery and technology. Having grown up almost in the shadow of the Ardnacrusha power station, hearing Dad's stories of his involvement in building it, I have great admiration for the vision and technical skills of the people involved in its creation. When Ireland was barely beginning to understand the implications of independence, and was still recovering from years of war, our government took the bold step of funding and creating what was for a time the most modern, sophisticated hydroelectric plant in the world.

Today, a hundred years on, Ardnacrusha power station is still an awesome sight. Yet, ironically, the best way that we can honour the vision of its creators would be to decommission the power station. Its builders were striving to modernise Ireland, to utilise our natural resources to enable a comfortable, sustainable way of life for everyone who lives here. Now, we need to completely reimagine our relationship with the Shannon and with all the species that live in it. First Ardnacrusha, and then every hydroelectric plant in the North Atlantic region.

I believe that the decommissioning of Ardnacrusha and all of its associated works would be very much in the spirit in which it was originally constructed. Ardnacrusha's engineers had a vision for Ireland taking its place among the modern countries of the world, and even becoming an innovator and a leader. In 1925, that meant harnessing the incredible power of the River Shannon to make electricity, despite the damage to the natural environment.

But in the twenty-first century, that same urge to modernise, to innovate and to provide leadership can be realised in a different way. It can be realised by putting the environment first, for a change. By recognising that how we did things in the past is not necessarily how we should be doing them now. By taking a step as big and bold as that taken by the Irish Free State when it placed all its faith in the Shannon Scheme. We know what we have to do.

* * *

The Atlantic wild salmon is an iconic species in Ireland. It is part of who we are as a people, and it is a key species in the complex jigsaw that is our natural environment. By taking immediate steps to save it from extinction, we will also make Irish waters safer and healthier for innumerable other species – including, of course, our own. This must take place hand in hand with urgent measures to reduce, and ultimately eliminate, the ongoing pollution of our natural environment.

Reversing the Shannon Scheme, forging unprecedented levels of international cooperation, and giving the Atlantic wild salmon and the rest of nature a fighting chance, is a vital step. And I believe that we can do it. Someone has to take the first steps to save the Atlantic salmon, and it might as well be Ireland. After all, we have a lot to lose and a lot to gain, both environmentally and commercially.

All my life, my comings and goings from the Shannon have shadowed those of the salmon. Looking back at it now, I can clearly see that the Shannon and all the living beings it supports has been the great love of my life. I also know that I have counterparts all over the Atlantic region – men and women who grew up in traditional fisheries, who have seen their way of life change beyond recognition and their keystone species all but disappear from the water. I hope we can all work together to bring back the Atlantic wild salmon. In the process, the entire ecosystem of the North Atlantic will be improved, and traditional fishing communities that have collapsed will be given a chance to engage in lawful, small-scale, non-commercial fishing in a way that respects their ancestral customs, the needs of the salmon and the future environmental health of the Atlantic region.

I have had a great life – a truly wonderful life – and I regret none of the decisions that I have made along the way, or the places they have taken me.

But I do have my sorrows. As I write, I am entering the final decades of my existence, just as the Atlantic wild salmon are collectively entering theirs – unless something radical is done to prevent this environmental tragedy from taking place.

I have outlined a plan that could work, that could revive the numbers of wild salmon, and help to restore the health of the Shannon, and of our rivers and seas beyond the Shannon. The rest is up to you, and I wish you the very best of good luck. All I want, as a member of the last generation of traditional fishermen from my home village of Coonagh, is to reach the end of my life knowing I have done my best to save from extinction a species that has given me everything.

Notes

1 Bielenberg, 1997, 43.

2 Williams, 1835, 64; 74; 43–45.

3 'Project Discussed, How the Free State Would Benefit,' Freeman's Journal, 8 March 1924.

4 Bielenberg, 1997, 44.

5 Schoen, 2002, 41.

6 Fletcher, 1929, 490.

7 Duffy, 2017, 200.

8 *Leinster Reporter,* 19 March 1927.

9 McCarthy, 1957, 539–40.

10 O'Brien, 2017, vii.

11 Fletcher, 1929, 486.

12 O'Brien, 2017, 54.

13 Ardnacrusha Generating Station, ESB Publication, https://cdn.esb.ie/media/docs/default-source/education-hub/ardnacrusha-power-station.pdf?sfvrsn=38c739f0_0 Retrieved 23 August 2023.

14 Clancy, 2006, 28.

15 Duffy, 2017, 200–203.

16 McCarthy, 2002, 49.

17 *Nottingham and Midland Catholic News*, 29 May 1926.

18 McCarthy, 2002, 48.

19 Bielenberg, 1997, 47.

20 'Galway Visitors at Shannon Works, Successful Excursion,' *Galway Observer*, 23 June 1928.

21 Fletcher, 1929, 493–494.

22 Netboy, 1980, 109.

23 Bielenberg, 1997, 45.

24 Lawler, 1967, 409.

25 For example, *Sheffield Daily Telegraph*, 20 November 1929.

26 *The Sphere*, 1 October 1927.

27 *Ibid.*, 9 January 1929.

28 Delany, 2002, 19.

29 *Frontier Sentinel*, 15 December 1928.

30 Larmour, 2009, 13.

31 'All-Electric State, Shannon Waters Diverted to Feed Irish Turbines,' *Daily Herald*, 23 July 1929.

32 O'Brien, 2017, 199; 211–220.

33 *Ibid.*, 1.

34 Schoen, 2002, 46,

35 Murphy, 2012, 75–80.

36 Bielenberg, 1997, 47.

37 Inland Fisheries of Ireland, No. 8 Limerick District, 1930.

38 Netboy, 1980, 20.

39 NASCO, 2019, 24.

40 Went, 1981, 107–109.

41 Maxwell, 1832, 48.

42 Went, 1981, 107–110.

43 Netboy, 1980, 111.

44 *Ibid.*

45 Went, 1981, 113.

46 NASCO, 2019, 28.

47 Windsor *et al.*, 2012, 1.

48 Netboy, 1980, 42.

49 Went, 1946, 11.

50 Duffy, 2017, 205.

51 Cullen, 2002, 145.

52 Inland Fisheries of Ireland, No. 8 Limerick District, 16 February 1927.

53 Inland Fisheries of Ireland, No. 8 Limerick District, 12 May 1926.

54 Minute book of Limerick no. 8 fishery district, minutes of board meeting 16 February 1927, Limerick County Library Local Studies Department.

55 'Another Affray at Coonagh, Volley of Stones from the Shore,' *Munster News*, 2 May 1925; 'Fishermen and Bailiffs, Another Affray at Coonagh, Volleys of Stones from the Shore,' *Munster News*, 2 May 1925.

56 *Northern Whig*, 20 February 1926.

57 Inland Fisheries of Ireland, No. 8 Limerick District, Minute Book.

58 Went, 1946, 167.

59 Clancy, 2006, 30–31.

60 *Ibid.*, 25.

61 'City Items of Interest,' *Limerick Echo*, 21 January 1930.

62 https://www.irishstatutebook.ie/eli/1925/act/26/section/16/enacted/en/html#sec16.

Retrieved 28 May 2024.

63 Lysaght, 1964, 22.

64 Clancy, 2006, 22.

65 Lysaght, 1964, 21–22.

66 'Fishermen Clash with Bailiffs in Prohibited Water, Midnight Scenes on the Shannon,' *Irish Independent*, 13 July 1932.

67 *Ibid.*

68 'Shannon Fishery Dispute, Ministers' Proposals Considered Useless by Fishermen,' *Irish Independent*, 18 July 1932.

69 80 'Fishermen Clash with Bailiffs in Prohibited Water, Midnight Scenes on the Shannon,' *Irish Independent*, 13 July 1932.

70 Lysaght, 1964, 32.

71 Duffy, 2017, 205–206.

72 Cullen, 2002, 146.

73 *Ibid.*

74 National Folklore Collection, Schools' Collection, Vol. 597, p. 209.

75 *Ibid.*, Vol. 598, 51.

76 *Ibid.*, Vol. 597, 217.

77 Went, 1964, 191.

78 Nolan, 1901, 113. P. 1901 'Galway Castles and Owners in 1574.' *Journal of the Galway Archaeological & Historical Society*, Vol. 1 (1900–01), p. 113.

79 Mac Cárthaigh, 2011, 165.

80 'Murder of German, Ex-Soldier Sentenced to Death in Dublin,' *Irish Weekly and Ulster Examiner*, 23 March 1929.

81 'Condemned Man's Last Words to Warders,' *Northern Whig*, 26 April 1929.

82 McCrohan, 2008, xvii.

83 '£35,000 Fish Weir on the Shannon,' *Irish Independent*, 26 January 1940.

84 'More People Using Electricity,' 28 July 1942.

85 'Shannon Fisheries,' *Irish Weekly and Ulster Examiner*, 12 August 1944.

86 Went, 1946, 163.

87 Mathers *et al.*, 2002, 70.

88 Delany, 2002, 25.

89 Dempsey *et al.*, 2000, 189.

90 Clancy, 2006, 36.

91 Inland Fisheries of Ireland, No. 8 Limerick District, Minute Book, 25 October 1929.

92 *Ibid.*

93 *Ibid.*, 113.

94 Maxwell, 1832, 47.

95 *Ibid.*

96 Netboy, 1980, 89.

97 Salmon Research Trust of Ireland Incorporated, 1982, 8.

98 ESB, *The Shannon Fishery*, n.d., 21; 23.

99 Grimes 2015, 13.

100 NASCO Steering Committee, 2017, 203.

101 Dempsey *et al.*, 2000, 189.

102 Netboy, 1980, 46.

103 *Ibid.*

104 Dempsey *et al.*, 2000, 190.

105 Netboy, 1980, 108.

106 'New Proposals to Save Salmon,' *The Field*, 30 May 1979, 1182–1183.

107 'Ireland's First Big Air Rally for Limerick,' *Irish Independent,* 20 May 1948.

108 Salmon Research Trust of Ireland Incorporated, The, 1982, 32.

109 Young, 2017, 19.

110 Charney, 1994, 882.

111 'Burtonport Counts Cost of Salmon War,' *The Irish Times*, 21 July 1983.

112 'New Clashes Feared in Salmon War,' *Cork Examiner*, 20 July 1983.

113 'Compensation for Salmon Men?' *The Irish Skipper,* March 1987, 1.

114 'Irish Trawler Held by British off Rockall,' *The Irish Times*, 21 August, 1987.

115 'Fanad Fisheries,' *Derry Journal*, 7 April 1987.

116 'Board Calls for End to Off-Shore Salmon Fishing,' *Clare Champion*, 16 January 1987.

117 'The Call for a Cull;' 'Fishery Board to Campaign for a Sea Cull,' *The Irish Skipper*, 3, 5.

118 'Central Board Wants to End Salmon Drifting,' *The Irish Skipper*, February 1987, 18.

119 'Angry Reaction to Call for Drift-Net Ban,' *Derry People and Donegal News*, 10 January 1987.

120 For example, 'Fishing Wisdom,' *Irish Press*, 8 January 1987.

121 'Condoms River 'A Disgrace,' *Sunday World*, 19 June 1988, 10.

122 'Two Areas for Sea Farms,' *The Irish Skipper,* March 1987, 7.

123 'A Fine Catch for the ESB,' *The Irish Times*, 25 October 1988.

124 https://esbarchives.ie/wp-content/uploads/2016/02/esb-annual-reports_1988.pdf Retrieved 27 September 2023.

125 Dempsey *at al.*, 2000, 190.

126 'Taking a Businesslike Approach to Growth,' *The Irish Times*, 25 October 1988.

127 *Ibid.*

128 Nasco, 2019, 6.

129 https://www.irishtimes.com/news/settlement-in-ballycotton-case-1.27416
130 https://www.irishexaminer.com/news/arid-20124245.html.
131 https://esbarchives.ie/wp-content/uploads/2016/02/esb-annual-reports_1991.pdf.
132 https://esbarchives.ie/wp-content/uploads/2016/02/esb-annual-reports_1993.pdf.
133 https://www.oireachtas.ie/en/debates/debate/dail/1995-02-15/82/ Retrieved 27 September 2023.
134 'State Plan to Conserve Wild Salmon runs into Shallows,' *The Irish Times*, 24 May 1999.
135 Cullen, 2002, 152.
136 See Kerr *et al.*, 2015 for a discussion of Armand-Delille and his introduction of the disease.
137 Siggins, Lorna, 'Buyout of Drift-net Rights "not workable",' *The Irish Times*, 6 November 2000.
138 'Conserving Salmon,' *The Irish Times* editorial, 18 July 200.
139 Siggins, Lorna, 'Fahey Suffers Setback as Salmon Commission Chair Resigns,' *The Irish Times*, 16 March 2001.
140 'Call To End Indiscriminate Ocean Driftnetting,' An Angler's Viewpoint, *Irish Independent*, 30 September 2002.
141 Sheahan, Fionnán, 'Minister Acts Against Salmon Firm,' *Irish Examiner*, 22 September 2003.
142 Hogan, Treacy, 'Overfishing, Poison Wiping out Salmon,' *Irish Independent*, 2 June 2001.
143 Jenkins, 2003, 844.
144 *Ibid.*, 845.
145 'Bumper Catches Reveal Wild Salmon Crisis Here,' *Sunday Independent*, 5 December 2005.
146 'Fishermen Consider €80m Licence Buyout.' *Irish Independent*, 14 August 2004.
147 Lee, John. 'Netted,' *Ireland on Sunday*, 21 November 2004.
148 Windsor *et al.*, 2012, 1.
149 'Drift Net Claims Life of Basking Shark,' *The Irish Times*, 10 July 2007.
150 O'Malley, Joseph. 'The Salmon of Knowledge is not Like to be Found Lurking on the Back Bench,' *The Irish Times*, 29 October 2006.
151 'Drift Netting Threatens Salmon Stocks and Tourist Industry,' Letters to the Editor, *Irish Examiner*, 16 March 2006.
152 160 Lee, John. 'Last Act as Fisheries Minister – Handout for Constituents; Fury over Cope's €4m For His Own Back Yard, *Ireland on Sunday*, 19 February 2006.
153 Evans, Derek, 'The Drift-net Threat,' Angling Notes, Time Out, *The Irish Times*, 8 October 2007.

154 NASCO, 2019, 6.

155 Richards *et al.*, 2020.

156 Windsor *et al.*, 2012, 11.

157 https://www.marine.ie/site-area/areas-activity/aquaculture/sea-lice/sea-lice. Retrieved 28 August 2013.

158 Windsor *et al.*, 2012, 13.

159 NASCO, 2019, 6.

160 'Salmon Farmers "Put Wild Fish at Risk in Fight to Kill off Sea Lice",' *The Observer*, 7 June 2017.

161 'Working Group to Improve Shannon River Fish Passages,' *Limerick Leader*, 27 October 2018.

162 https://www.fao.org/state-of-fisheries-aquaculture#. Retrieved 29 August 2023.

163 NASCO, 2019, 11.

164 Fraser, 2017, 11.

165 Changing Markets Foundation, 2019, 11.

166 *Ibid.*, 2019, 61.

167 https://www.eca.europa.eu/en/publications?did=57066. Retrieved 29 August 2023.

168 https://www.vitenskapsradet.no/Nyheter/Status-of-wild-Atlantic-salmon-in-norway-2023. Retrieved 18 October 2023.

169 https://www.noteworthy.ie/shall-not-pass-abstraction-law-6011223-Mar2023/; https://www.oireachtas.ie/en/debates/debate/dail/2022-12-08/37/. Retrieved 28 May 2024.

170 'Eamon Ryan Removes Remaining Three Board Members of Inland Fisheries Ireland,' *The Irish Times*, 14 February 2023.

171 NASCO, 2019, 19.

Bibliography

Bielenberg, Andy. 'Keating & the Shannon Scheme,' *History Ireland, Autumn 1997, Vol. 5, No. 3, 43–47.*

Bielenberg, Andy (ed.). *The Shannon Scheme and the Electrification of the Irish Free State*, The Lilliput Press, 2002.

Changing Markets Foundation, Fishing for Catastrophe, 2019, https://changingmar-kets.org/wp-content/uploads/2019/10/CM-WEB-FINAL-FISHING-FOR-CA-TASTROPHE-2019.pdf. Retrieved 29 August 2023.

Charney, Jonathan I. 'The Marine Environment and the 1982 United Nations Convention on the Law of the Sea,' *The International Lawyer*, Winter 1994, Vol. 28, No. 4, 879–901.

Clancy, Sharon. *The Abbey Fishermen: History and Culture of a Fishing Community*, Trafford Publishing, 2006.

Coonagh War Memorial Committee. *From Coonagh to the Dardanelles: Gandelows, Liners and Battleships,* 2015.

Cullen, Bob. 'Some Notable Features of the Design and Operational History of Ardnacrusha Since 1929,' in Bielenberg, 2002, 138–154.

Delaney, Brendan. 'McLaughlin, the Genesis of the Shannon Scheme and the ESB,' in Bielenberg, 2002, 11–28, 19.

Dempsey, Suzanne; Costello, Mark J; Quigley, Declan; Warrer-Hansen, Ivar; Briody, Mary; Thompson, Enda; and Gillooly, Michael. 'Freshwater Salmon and Trout Farm Characteristics and Production in Ireland,' *Internationale Vereinigung für Theoretische und Angewandte Limnologie: Verhandlungen, 2000,* Vol. 27, No. 1, 189–193.

Duffy, Paul. 'Rishworth, McLaughlin and the Shannon Scheme,' *Journal of the Galway Archaeological and Historical Society*, Vol. 69 (2017), 195–215.

Electricity Supply Board. *The Shannon Fishery* [Date not given, but clearly approx. 1970 as last date in text refers to 1969].

Fletcher, George. 'The Shannon Scheme and its Economic Consequences,' *Journal of the Royal Society of Arts*, 1929, Vol. 77, No. 3983.

Fraser, Dylan J. 'Risks and Benefits to Atlantic Wild Salmon Populations from Hatchery and Stocking Activities, with Particular Emphasis on Smolt-to-Adult Captive-Reared Supplementation,' in NASCO, 2017, 7–16.

Grimes, Mike. 'Salmon Fishing and Reed Harvesting,' in *Coonagh War Memorial Committee*, 2015, 11–15.

Inland Fisheries Trust and Bord Fáilte Éireann. *Ireland: Salmon and Sea Trout Fishing,* 1964.

Jenkins, David. *'Atlantic Salmon, Endangered Species, and the Failure of Environmental Policies,' Comparative Studies in Society and History,* 2003, Vol. 45, No. 4, 843–872.

Kelly, Eamonn P. 'A Log-boat From Clenagh, Co. Clare,' *North Munster Antiquarian Journal,* 1987, Vo. 29, 93–94.

Kerr, Peter J; Liu, June; Cattadori, Isabella; *et al.* 'Myxoma Virus and the Leporipoxviruses: An Evolutionary Paradigm,' *Viruses,* 2015 vol. 7, no. 3, pp 1020–1061.

Larmour, Paul. *Free State Architecture: Modern Movement Architecture in Ireland, 1922–1949,* Gandon Editions, 2009.

Lawler, Edward A. 'The Electricity Supply Board: 40th Anniversary,' *An Irish Quarterly Review, 1967, Vol. 56, No. 224, 406–413.*

Lenihan, Maurice. *Limerick: Its History and Antiquities,* Hodges, Smith, 1866.

Lysaght, William. *The Abbey Fishermen: A Short History,* The Treaty Press. 1964.

Mathers, RG; De Carlos, M; Crowley, K; and Ó Teangana, D. 'A Review of the Potential Effect of Irish Hydroelectric Installations on Atlantic Salmon (*Salmo salar L.*) Populations, with Particular Reference to the River Erne,' *Biology and Environment: Proceedings of the Royal Irish Academy,* 2002, Vol. 102B, 69–79.

Maxwell, WH. *Wild Sports of the West of Ireland,* Routledge and Sons, *1832.*

Mac Cárthaigh, Críostóir. 'Turf Boats and Turf Cots of the Shannon Estuary,' *Béaloideas, Iml. 79* (2011), 165–175.

McCarthy, Albert JP. 'The Irish National Electrification Scheme,' *Geographical Review,* Oct., 1957, Vol. 47, No. 4, 539–554.

McCarthy, Michael. 'How the Shannon Scheme Workers Lived,' in Bielenberg 2002, 48–72.

McCrohan, Owen. *Paddy Mo, the Life of Patrick Moriarty, 1926–1997,* The Lilliput Press, 2008.

McHugh, FD. 'Where the River Shannon Flows,' *Scientific American,* May 1929, Vol. 140, No. 5, 400–403.

Murphy, Charlotte. 'Limerick and the Eucharistic Congress, 1932,' *North Munster Antiquarian Journal,* 2012, Vol. 52, 75–80.

Netboy, Anthony. *Salmon; the World's Most Harassed Fish,* Andre Deutsch, 1980.

Nolan, JP. 1901 'Galway Castles and Owners in 1574,' *Journal of the Galway Archaeological & Historical Society,* 1900–1901, Vol. 1.

North Atlantic Salmon Conservation Organization (NASCO). *Understanding the Risks and Benefits of Hatchery and Stocking Activities to Atlantic Wild Salmon Populations,* Report of a Theme-Based Special Session of the Council of NASCO, Wednesday 7 June 2017, Varberg, Sweden.

North Atlantic Salmon Conservation Organisation (NASCO) Steering Committee. *Conclusions of the Steering Committee*, NASCO, 2017, 97–107.

North Atlantic Salmon Conservation Organization (NASCO). *State of North Atlantic Salmon*, Report, 2019.

O'Brien, Sorcha. *Powering the Nation: Images of the Shannon Scheme and Electricity in Ireland*, Irish Academic Press, 2017.

Richards, John L; Sheng, Victoria; Yi, Chung Wing; Ying, Chan Lai; Ting, Ng Sin; Sadovy, Yvonne; and Baker, David. 'Prevalence of critically endangered European eel (*Anguilla anguilla*) in Hong Kong Supermarkets,' *Science Advances*, Vol. 6, 20.

Salmon Research Trust of Ireland Incorporated, The. *Annual Report No XXVII*, Arthur Guinness Son and Co Ltd., and the Minister for Agriculture and Fisheries, 1982.

Schoen, Lother. 'The Irish Free State and the Electricity Industry, 1922–1927,' in Bielenberg, 2002, 28–47, 41.

Went, Arthur EJ. 'Salmon of the River Shannon in 1944 and 1945,' *Journal of Animal Ecology*, 1946, Vol. 15, No. 2, 155–169.

Went, Arthur EJ. 'The Pursuit of Salmon in Ireland,' *Proceedings of the Royal Irish Academy: Archaeology, Culture, History, Literature,* 1962–1964, Vol. 63, 191–244.

Went, Arthur EJ. 'Historical Notes on the Fisheries of the Estuary of the River Shannon,' *The Journal of the Royal Society of Antiquaries of Ireland*, 1981, Vol. 111, 107–118.

Williams, CW. *CW Williams on Inland Navigation and the Application of Money Grant in Aid of Public Works*, Bain *et al.* publishers, 1835.

Windsor, Malcolm L; Hutchinson, Peter; Hansen, Lars Petter; and Redden, David D. 'Atlantic Salmon at Sea: Findings from Recent Research and their Implications for Management,' NASCO document CNL (12) 60.

Young, Kyle A. 'Approaches to Minimising Negative Consequences to Atlantic Wild Salmon Populations from Hatchery and Stocking Activities', NASCO 2017, 17–32.